Murder and Mystery

on

EXMOOR

Jack Hurley

The Exmoor Press

© Jack Hurley, 1971

Fourth (enlarged) edition, 1982

Reprinted 1991

ISBN 0 900131 40 3

MICROSTUDIES

Each Microstudy has been written by an expert and is designed to appeal to all who are interested in Exmoor.

A list of all the titles is available from

The Exmoor Press   Dulverton   Somerset

Front Cover: Illustration by Sally J. Maynard, The Old Blacksmith's Gallery, Dulverton.
Back Cover: Wheal Eliza Mine and Cottage (Colin Thornton).

Printed in Great Britain by Williton Printers

Contents

Photographs

All the subjects are the work of Colin Thornton except those on pages 4, 22 and 41. Page 74 was taken by R. Priddy, and page 78 by David Frier.

Thanks are also due to the Curator of the Ilfracombe Museum for permission to reproduce the picture on page 70.

Drawing
by Diana C. Saunders.

The Author

JACK HURLEY was born at Williton in Somerset in 1913. After leaving the Richard Huish College at Taunton, he joined the staff of the *West Somerset Free Press* as a journalist, and retired as Editor in 1980, having completed 50 years with the paper. He contributed *Notes by the Way*, the paper's weekly feature on the life and traditions of West Somerset and Exmoor, a subject on which he was an acknowledged expert. In the Queen's Birthday Honours List in 1981 he was awarded the MBE for his services to the district through journalism. He is the author of four other titles published by the Exmoor Press — *Snow and Storm on Exmoor, Legends of Exmoor, Exmoor in Wartime*, and *Rattle his Bones* (an account of Exmoor Workhouses).

Jack Hurley died in 1983.

Wheal Eliza Cottage as it used to be.

Introduction

Murder and mystery set against Exmoor? One has a feeling that the stage backdrop is inappropriate.

For Exmoor wears such a serene, unshadowed countenance by comparison with darkly mysterious Dartmoor and its granite-capped tors.

A baying hound (a 'Baskerville', of course) seems right for a Dartmoor blood-curdle . . . and Conan Doyle knew it. Exmoor's only reply is the belling stag. Belligerent, perhaps, but a reassurance that all is well and natural in the Exmoor world.

Dartmoor offers the setting for fictional mystery which few writers would attempt to place on Exmoor. Here, one has to turn almost entirely to factual mystery, to the shadows superimposed on the moorland's pleasant face by human agency. Hence the stories in this book.

Three of them concern the discovery of bodies . . . one (established as murder) down a mine shaft, a second (self-destruction) in that Exmoor lake, Pinkery, a third in a bog.

And there is the difference. This one is the tragic story of Mollie Phillips, an Exford girl. It remains today an irritatingly inconclusive case. Was this girl, whose remains were found in a bog, destroyed by a natural feature of the moor, or does one look for human agency? Readers may be able to make up their minds. There are bound to be some who will 'exonerate' Exmoor.

Curiously, two of the stories, widely separated in time, have a kind of common denominator, the same brand of leading actor in the drama . . . an Exmoor parson. One held his nose to the scent of murder and never lifted it until the criminal was in a cell; the other raised the cry of 'murder' but listened in vain for the answering echoes from authority.

Then there are mysteries starting out as such, but which are probed and satisfactorily explained. Additionally, we have the creepy mysteries represented by the silent flit of an Exmoor phantom across the page. Try probing these, and one's finger goes right through the page!

Finally, there is the thing our ancestors liked to pretend was a mystery . . . simply because they chose not to look on it . . . smuggling. But they were not above taking anything that came their way through it.

The only mystery which Exmoor has truly grown in its soil is that of the Doones. It is the mystery of their existence or their creation. Which? A full examination of the question is beyond the scope of a chapter; therefore the Doones have been deliberately avoided in these pages. For their story see another title in the Microstudy Series, *The Lorna Doone Trail* by S. H. Burton.

1 The Blood of a Priest

The midsummer night was warm . . . or was there another reason for the beads that broke on Alice Walker's brow?

She was bending over the tub. The thing they had given her to do was about finished. The parboiled flesh was salted down. That ought to delay putrefaction and with it the loathsome smell that could give a twitch to the village nostril of suspicion.

It was not the flesh of a cottager's pig that Alice Walker had been salting.

. . . . . .

The problem is always with the murderer . . . what to do with the body. The modern annals of crime show examples varying from the clumsy to the cunning. Murderer John Haigh thought he had completely solved the business with a carbuoy of acid, and seemed rather proud to say so.

Alice Walker, Peter Smethwicke, Andrew Baker and Cyril Austen, 300 years before, had the disposal problem, from which they emerge as the gory principals in a hideous West Country crime.

Murder is murder, and in a moral analysis there can be no degrees. Yet human nature will always create them, according to the circumstances of the crime and the parties in the case. For instance, there is parracide, the killing of someone to whom reverence is considered to be due, and the murder of Archbishop Becket in 1170 is a supreme national example in the revulsion it evoked. Politically, it removed the King's 'troublesome priest'. In 1624, in a much lower strata of the ecclesia, a desperate band at Old Cleeve removed their own man of God because they considered him troublesome.

The deed itself was bad enough; the treatment of the corpse was a sheer horror. A contemporary recorder saw it as a crime 'scarce to be paralleled, except it be by the very cannibals and man-eating Tartars'.

Outspoken Minister

This was the murder of the Rev. Mr. Trat, the curate of Old Cleeve. This large parish has a northern border against the Bristol Channel; a southern boundary, and villages, inside the Exmoor National Park. Trat, who came into the curacy while the Rev. Edward Brickenden was Rector, quickly aroused the antagonism of a section of the flock because he was so instant in reproof of their sins.

They did not take his chidings lying down. Crafty attempts were made to discredit him as a minister. His wife had drowned when cut off by the tide on Cleeve's shore, and a malicious tale was put about that he had killed her. Ultimately, the magistracy investigated the allegation and found it baseless.

6

But Trat's enemies were resourceful. Next, they tried a mud-sling. Shameful in itself, in its contrivance it would not have disgraced the pages of a thriller. Someone put on Trat's gown and hat, prowled the highway until a woman came along, accosted her and attempted an assault. The effect was everything Trat's enemies had hoped for. The woman named Trat as her assailant, saying she had recognised his gown and hat.

The episode failed to weaken Trat's standing as a minister; his enemies must try yet again. They were numerous, but for the ultimate Trat removal act the field was narrowed to a few.

Turning On The Hate

Among several young fellows who had crossed swords with Trat was Peter Smethwicke, grandson of Rector Brickenden. The Rector was about to resign the living in favour of Trat, and this would give the curate a bigger standing. Smethwicke was smarting over this, but then something else turned on his deadly hatred. The Rector had promised him the perpetual patronage of the Old Cleeve living, but sold it to Trat.

Smethwicke determined that the troublesome curate must redress this wrong with his own death. He laid his plans, and it is apparent that his father was party to them. (The elder Smethwicke's Christian name seems to have been lost in the passage of time.) Peter Smethwicke picked up accomplices . . . Andrew Baker and Cyril Austen . . . and they would ultimately involve a woman.

Trat got around the district on horseback. On the Wednesday following Midsummer Day he took his last ride. Smethwicke, Baker and Austen were lying in wait off the highway. They sprang, unhorsed the curate and stabbed him to death.

Mutilation

Since the death of his wife Trat had lived alone, and it was to his own house that the murderers carried the corpse. There they cut off the head and burned it, amputated Trat's arms and legs, and disembowled him like a pig. The limbs were broken up and crushed into fragments which, with the bowels, were stowed in earthen pots. The remainder of the body was parboiled and put in a salter, a cue for Alice Walker to roll up her sleeves and perform her grisly chore. A servant in the Smethwickes' house, Alice was probably privy to the murder plan, and she was known to have detested Trat.

What was done to the corpse, especially severing and burning the head, was purposeful . . . sickeningly in step with so much else that had gone on between Trat and his enemies. His remains were bound to be discovered sooner or later, but what if it were impossible to identify them as his? The head was gone; all else was fragmented.

Then let Trat be still alive . . . somewhere. And let it be put about that the remains must be those of a poor wanderer whom Trat, the monster-minister, had enticed inside to murder and mangle.

The Bluff

This was where Smethwicke the elder came in, and he literally went some way toward pulling off the bluff. He began to move through the county dressed in Trat's hat and coat, stopping here and there to drop a hint that he was Curate Trat, of Old Cleeve. He laid his false trail from Old Cleeve to Taunton, to Ilchester, and over the border into Dorset.

A fortnight after the murder, Trat's disappearance having been reported meanwhile, law officers broke into the house and found the ghastly evidences of crime. The first clue was found in the house . . . a coat belonging to Peter Smethwicke. The inquiries moved to the Smethwickes' house, and the first person to be detained on suspicion was Alice Walker. This prompted Smethwicke the elder into his desperate throw. He declared that the remains found in Trat's house must be those of a wanderer whom the curate had murdered. Smethwicke, as already stated, then went off on his red herring travels as 'Mr. Trat'.

If he hoped to draw the law after him and away from his son Peter, he was mistaken. The officers hung around the Smethwicke house. And in it they came across sickening clues . . . charred pieces of skull bone and a pot full of blood.

He Dropped It

Andrew Baker was in the house at the time. When the officers asked him to pick up the pot of blood and he appeared deliberately to drop it, they assumed he must know a thing or two. He became their second detainee. Peter Smethwicke was the third. Cyril Austen had skipped to another part of the county, but in his possession was a bloodstained piece of cloth. Someone saw it, spread the news, and the law's arm, pretty long, even in those days, reached out from Old Cleeve. The days of the elder Smethwicke's travels as a bogus curate were running out, and he was duly added to the tally to complete an appallingly evil bunch of malefactors.

Justice Tanfield listened to the evidence at the Somerset Assize. The elder Smethwicke was sent back to gaol pending the production of further evidence against him, and the records seem to be silent as to his eventual fate. Peter Smethwicke, Alice Walker, Baker and Austen, were found guilty and sentenced to death.

Refusing to confess their guilt, they were written off as obstinate and unrepentant sinners. On the morning of July 25 they looked their last upon the earthly scene from the cross-beam at Stonegallows, just west of Taunton.

Shattering to reflect that the law, in the penalties it exacted, once made no distinction between the sheep-stealer and the four unspeakables who dangled at Stonegallows that morning.

8

2 Who Killed The Conibeers?

A frenzied flailing arm, a hacking, bloody blade. Not one corpse, but three.

It might be under the lights of a film studio, with Alfred Hitchcock directing.

But this triple, hideous butchery was in the light of a June sun.

Lying along the eastern perimeter of the Exmoor National Park, on the Wiveliscombe—Watchet road, a mile north of Monksilver village, is the hamlet of Woodford. Its dwellings include one which has been attractively modernised and was originally a cottage of the Jacobean period.

Here in 1773 were living a family of three women, Mrs. Elizabeth Conibeer, aged 88, and her two daughters, Anne, 45, and Sarah, 43.

Death in the appalling guise of a madman (he could have been nothing less) struck them down at noontide on June 5th. They were eating their dinner in the kitchen. They were expecting a caller . . . the baker's boy, and a little pile of pence lay on the table for him to collect.

The cottage door stood open to the warm sunshine.

Suddenly, soundlessly, a monster was through that door and into the kitchen. A blade flashed and fell at the impulse of a berserk brain, and in moment three forms lay huddled on the floor in a welter of blood.

An attack of such swift, extreme savagery that it gave not one of the victims a chance of evasion. Perhaps not even a chance for a full scream before it was choked in the women's throats by the slashing knife.

Because a hundred yards away, the baker's lad, approaching in his cart, heard nothing. He stopped outside the cottage and carried his loaves to the door. It now stood half open.

The horror inside petrified him, but only for a moment, and he turned, ran to his cart and drove off to raise the alarm.

Lucky for him that he did not linger; it seems probable that the murderer was at that moment concealed behind the door.

Elizabeth Conibeer lay between her daughters. Blood was everywhere; on the table with the meal, staining the floor with patches that for years resisted attempts at erasure.

The crime was never brought home to anyone. Even the finger of suspicion failed to straighten in any particular direction. For the complete absence of clue to this deed, or possible motive, that

In Memory
of Mrs ELIZABETH CONIBEER
Aged Eighty Eight Years.
And her two Daughters. ANN aged
Forty five, and SARAH Forty three
who was all Inhumanly Murdered
in the Day of the Fifth of June 1775
In their House at Woodford,
in this Parish.

Inhuman Wretch who e'er thou art
That didst commit this hainous Crime
Repent before thou dost depart
To meet thine Awfull Judge Divine.

Tomb of the Conibeers in Monksilver Churchyard.

knife might as well have been wielded by a fiendish escapee from hell.

The Conibeers were buried in the churchyard at Monksilver, a mile along the road.

Their tomb is still to be seen, and if some awful fascination ever drew their murderer to it, these are the words that would have leapt across to him from the stone:

Inhuman wretch, who'er thou art
That didst commit this hainous crime,
Repent, before thou dost depart
To meet thy awful Judge Divine.

But words about wrath to come were probably not the kind of confrontation to wring remorse from a soulless killer who was walking free.

3 Gibbet on the Common

He hung handsome in death. Everybody who came to see him in his first week aloft noted this strange thing. The undistorted countenance retained the pink hue of health and life.

The country folk were glad, for they had liked this young fellow. Now he was dead . . . but without looking it, so kind was death to his features. Almost as if death was a person who shared the people's liking for this man.

Decomposition may have delayed its attack, but inevitably it must start. And as this man would go on hanging in a cage, month after month, the developing spectacle would not be pretty.

But for the moment John Walford, hanging high, was hanging handsome. That consoled his friends.

. . . . . .

Brutal murder, committed in a roughish time. Strangely, this one did not arouse the passions of a roughish time . . . no mob anger, no howl of execration during the final scenes around the gibbet. Local people shied from calling this crime by its name. When they spoke of it, and especially of the man concerned, it was more in sorrow. The case was expressed, in a kindly euphemism, as 'the tragedy of the hills', and that is how it passed down through the generations.

It added a place-name to the many of local interest that are to be found on Exmoor and the Quantock Hills. The great majority are of happy association, but Quantock gives us Dead Woman's Ditch . . . meaning precisely what it says. In that ditch had lain the body of the woman John Walford killed after being married to her for less than a month.

The Collier

Many people think National Parks legislation should have put the Quantocks in with Exmoor. These gracefully contoured hills, with their bosomly cleft of combe, were the home ground and workplace of John Walford. They provided his solitude . . . too much of it . . . and they provided his temptation.

And when he was 24 years of age they provided his gallows. Here was a man who killed, yet was not cursed. What had he about him that he should come down in story as 'the likeable murderer'?

He was born at Over Stowey in 1765. The family had been settled there for generations. Walford made a living as a collier or charcoal burner, and during the summers he was a part-time helper on local farms. He could neither read nor write, which did not mean that he lacked intelligence; indeed, he projected a quality that suggested he might have gone far if the benefits of education had been his.

Walford was a presentable fellow, dark and handsome. He was a good worker, the farmers he helped thought highly of him, and his mates knew him as good company. His summers in the fields were happy; his winters gloomy, for then he became the charcoal burner in the woods, a job that kept him from his home and society from one weekend to the next. He had built a little cone-shaped shelter with poles and turf, and inside was a bed of straw. Every Saturday he returned home, changed his clothes, removed his grime, and drank ale with his friends. On Sunday he went to church. On Monday it was back to the hut and the loneliness.

The young man thought often and tenderly of Ann Rice, an Over Stowey miller's daughter, and she similarly of him. There was an understanding that one day they would marry.

The Other Girl

Fate approached Walford in the person of a girl called Jenny. Squabby and plain, slovenly dressed, none too clean, and sharp without being intelligent, she moved across the hills from Stowey, gathering bundles of sticks. Walford often saw her, and one day she came too close to a man who lived with loneliness all the week and was healthily hungry for more than bread.

Jenny, underneath the rags, was a woman. Inevitably, Walford got her with child, which brought trouble for him from the parish overseers. Jenny visited him many times in his hut. Never by invitation. That, he always maintained. The visits produced a second child. This time the parish officers arrested him. He obtained his release by promising to marry the girl. Even so, the officers were sorry that the popular John Walford was having to sacrifice himself!

On June 18th, 1789, Walford married Jenny; on July 5th he killed her.

Late Night Walk

From the start of his association with Jenny, Walford had glimpsed his own downfall. 'She is doomed to be my ruin', he had been heard to say. Had he been resigned to making the best of a bad job, he might have avoided tragedy. But that was not John Walford. He had too much spirit and it told him he need not lie on the bed he had made. He thought of leaving the district. He mentioned this to a close friend and asked him to go as well. Walford was thinking of London. They looked at their money . . . and realised the idea was stillborn.

Walford always maintained that he did not premeditate his wife's murder. Late on the night of Saturday, July 5, Jenny said she wanted to go to the Castle of Comfort public house to buy cider. Walford gave her a shilling and told her to go along, but she said she was afraid to walk alone at this hour. She prevailed on Walford to accompany her.

That was her fatal mistake. On the way they quarrelled and Walford, seizing a stick, struck her a blow on the head which knocked her to the ground. It was as he saw her lying there that the devil put it into his head (those words were in his statement) to finish the job. Had he been able to do what he intended, he might have been walking free . . . as a man whose wife had disappeared without trace. For it occurred to him to tumble Jenny down a nearby mineshaft. But she was very heavy and he could hardly move her. So with his clasp-knife he slashed her throat, and as effectively as if he had been a butcher. Before he could skip away, her blood spurted over his clothes.

Was it a ghoulish meanness that made Walford search his dead wife's pocket for the shilling he had given her, or was the idea to remove a clue? Take the coin he did, and it was a killer's first mistake. He started back to his cottage, crossing a common and then passing along a lane where the arching trees must have seemed to close the horror of his deed in upon him. To reach his door he had to pass under his neighbours' windows, and so that he might not be heard he slipped off his shoes.

Inside his cottage he stripped himself naked and washed the blood from his hands and clothes. He spread the articles to dry, lay down naked on the bed, and when dawn came he dressed in his Sunday clothes . . . and waited.

The Shilling Clue

It was not a long wait. Jenny's body was found before 7 a.m., and people were soon hammering on Walford's door. He made a show of surprise at their news and said he had given his wife a shilling to go to the Castle of Comfort and she had not returned.

Then why had he not gone to look for her? they asked. He answered, foolishly, that he would not have known where to go.

13

Then, leaving the house, he met his brother William, to whom he made the amazing remark that Jenny had 'done a good chore' . . . she had cut her throat!

A small party went with Walford to see the body. He must have known they were a closing ring. When he saw the body he feigned shock and fell back upon a bank to rest, but he was thinking hard. He repeated the true story of giving his wife a shilling, and now he bent and searched her pocket for it. When he drew blank he had his cue for saying that someone must have accosted his wife, then robbed and killed her.

An examination of Walford's cottage was quickly productive of his clasp-knife, not entirely free from bloodstain, and stockings with bits of sand and gravel on the feet. In a sense, Walford was undone by his breeches! These were produced, and from a pocket fell a shilling. He had forgotten to remove it when he took off his breeches the night before.

The game was up. From the start, Walford had never held a decent card.

The Weeping Judge

It was not yet ten o'clock, but Walford was in custody and on his way to Nether Stowey and the lock-up. The following morning the coroner's inquest was held on the body of Jenny. When her head was scalped it was revealed that her skull had been fractured by the blow she took before her throat was cut. The jury returned a verdict of 'Wilful Murder, perpetrated by John Walford'.

He came to trial at the Somerset Assize at Bridgwater on August 18, 1789. The judge was Lord Kenyon. Now, in the penultimate act of 'the tragedy of the hills', Walford projected his old image to the people who packed the courtroom. Friends testified to his general good temper and character. The mind's eye showed them, not a brutal young killer, but the handsome fellow they had all liked . . . the popular John for whom life had gone awry. Life was to blame, not John Walford! Lord Kenyon wept copiously when he pronounced the death sentence.

Walford had pleaded not guilty, but in the condemned cell he confessed his crime. He insisted that he had killed his wife without the least premeditation.

Just one voice was raised against him. Cried the dead woman's mother: 'I shall go to see the murderous dog hanged'. So would a great crowd of people, but not in that frame of mind. It was directed that Walford should be hanged on the hills at Dodington Common, and re-hung in chains after death.

Last Journey

On the morning of August 20, only 48 hours after his trial, Walford began his last journey . . . back to his own hills. Fettered hand and foot, he lay in a cart, and beside him was the cage in which his body would hang.

The cart stopped at Nether Stowey because word was brought that the gallows were not quite ready. Walford was taken to an inn, where he had a meal and drank some ale . . . giving the health of those around him. When it was time to proceed he asked if it was possible to stay just a little longer. A negative shaking of heads . . . and in a few moments Walford was again seated in the cart with his cage.

What of a girl mentioned earlier in this story? She may have been out of the focus of this record, but she had never been out of John Walford's mind. And now the past, and all that might have been, rose in front of the young man, for up to the cart came Ann Rice, the girl he had always loved. She climbed into the cart, and for a few moments Walford talked with her. Then officers drew Ann away and the cart creaked onward.

A strange thing happened. The horses stopped, without an order, at the murder spot. 'I see it', said Walford. 'Drive on'.

Now they were under the gallows tree. Walford asked if Ann Rice had followed the cart, and they brought her to him. She was almost lifeless in her distress. They lifted her into the cart, and there were a few last whispers. As the girl was gently removed, Walford attempted to kiss her, but an officer said: 'You had better not, it can do no good'.

Walford now stood in the cart with the rope around his neck. His last words were of confession, but that he never 'fore-intended' the murder. His face was hooded, and he dropped a handkerchief as a signal to the executioner. The cart was drawn away, and John Walford swung.

At public executions it was usual for the watching crowd to relieve nervous tension in a burst of execration directed at the dying criminal, and sometimes at the executioner. But as John Walford expired the crowd were silent. A depth of silence that threw up the natural and happy sounds . . . the twittering of birds in the woods, the buzz of bees in the heather.

When Walford was dead his body was taken down, placed in the iron cage, and re-suspended. He stayed handsome for the first week, and all his friends marvelled. After a year and a day the cage dropped, and it was buried, with Walford's remains, under the gallows tree.

Nearby, a new place-name, Dead Woman's Ditch, would take root.

4 A Shroud for Little Anna

Night has ears as well as eyes.

The man out on an Exmoor hillside on a night in June, 1858, was up to no good. For that reason he was reluctant at first to come forward and speak of what he had heard. Eventually he did. He had seen nothing; it was too dark. And he had heard nothing more than footsteps. But the very direction those footsteps were taking was suggestive . . . horribly so. They seemed to punctuate the sentences of macabre story.

From that moment the two and two of crime could be put together to make the four of fate, and the hangman's rope was virtually around the neck of William Burgess.

This was the man who perpetrated the foulest, most sickening murder in the crime annals of Exmoor. He killed his own child because she was costing him half a crown a week to keep in lodgings. When he considered what that money would buy him in liquor . . . well, little Anna Maria, aged seven, was definitely in the way.

Burgess put her out of the way on a Sunday morning and buried her on the moor. No practised sexton could have cut a neater grave.

But Anna did not lie in her grave more than two nights. Burgess, through what he may have considered a wretched stroke of ill-luck, was forced to disinter the body and dispose of it elsewhere. By so doing he attached to his dreadful crime the tag of The Wheal Eliza Murder.

Moving westward from Landacre Bridge will take a walker into one of the most romantic spots in the Barle Valley. Sheardon Water comes in from the left. In the centre of the valley rise the three steep knolls which include Cow Castle. From the right the White Water stream comes down a narrow combe. In a cottage up that combe lived William Burgess, his wife, and their three children, Tom, Emma and Anna.

The murder of Anna may not have taken place here, for Burgess, after the death of his wife in 1857, had gone into lodgings at Simonsbath, taking Anna with him and putting Tom and Emma into service on a farm at North Molton. Nevertheless, the Burgess cottage at White Water duly gained a reputation for being haunted.

Burgess was but one of a good many rough, hard drinking men in this area. He had a certain native cunning which, incidentally, brought him into contact with the parson of Exmoor, the Rev. W. H. Thornton, whose church had just been built at Simonsbath.

Burgess had come to see Thornton to make a 'touch'. He pitched a tale about having lost a pony and a pig and asked Thornton to prepare him a begging letter he could take round with the object of raising funds to make good his loss. This was quite a common custom of the times, known as a 'brief', but it was sometimes abused. Thornton accepted Burgess's story, helped him with the 'brief', and Burgess cashed in on the practical sympathies of the people. He spent the money on a glorious binge in the taverns.

Thornton discovered that he had been hoodwinked. Angrily, he mentally registered Burgess as a cunning rogue. Burgess had made his first mistake.

Human Quarry

In the grim events of the Wheal Eliza crime Exmoor was to find that it had in Thornton a hunting parson in a different sense. Thornton's quarry was Burgess. And Burgess, as he lay under sentence of death, was to tell the governor of the gaol that it was Parson Thornton who from the first had hunted him down.

When Mrs. Burgess died, Burgess took little Anna to lodge with him at Gallon House Cot, in Simonsbath, where the landlady was a Mrs. Marley. On a Sunday in June, 1858, early in the morning, Burgess left the lodgings with the child, telling Mrs. Marley he was going to take Anna to lodge with her grandmother at Porlock Weir. He had the child's spare clothes with him. He returned the same day without the child, and he himself vanished from the district the following Thursday.

Between Sunday and Thursday, Burgess had been occupied with a grisly task.

The first strands of a quickly closing web of suspicion were spun when someone remarked that clothes had been burned at the back of the Gallon House Inn. Mrs. Marley was called to the scene and she considered that a piece of scorched calico had belonged to little Anna Burgess's spare frock.

Casual Questions

At this point Parson Thornton steps on to the trail. With so much gossip circulating he took the sensible course. He sent Will Court, the local forester, on horseback to Porlock Weir to look up Burgess's mother. Thornton told Court to behave naturally, ask questions casually of the old lady, but to say nothing about the missing child; merely observe whether or not she was there.

Court came back with a tale that did not surprise Thornton. Burgess had indeed gone to his mother's home that Sunday, but the child was not with him. And since that day Mrs. Burgess had neither seen nor heard from her son.

Thornton continued with the initiative. He felt it was now a case of tracing Burgess and looking for a tiny grave. Thornton told the parish constable to go to Lynmouth to enquire for Burgess, who might have got on a boat and crossed to Wales. (This was just what he had done).

At the same time Thornton told Forester Court to organise a

party to search the moors for the missing child. He meant: 'Look for a grave'.

Still Thornton was not done. He rode his horse to Curry Rivel, on the other side of Taunton, where lived the chief superintendent of police, Mr. Jeffs. Thornton rode through the night, caught the superintendent at 8 a.m. in the act of shaving, and prevailed on him to ride at once to Simonsbath.

When parson and police officer arrived they were told that a grave had been found. But it was empty!

The grave was about a mile from Gallon House Inn, along the line of some old mining trenches leading to the abandoned Wheal Eliza iron mine in the valley.

Why was it empty? One man knew . . . William Burgess. He must have cursed his ill-luck and the prevalence of sheep-stealing, which was another capital crime in those days. Sometimes sheep stealers would temporarily inter the carcase until a favourable opportunity for its removal and distribution presented itself. Two men had come across the grave in which Anna Burgess lay. They concluded that a slaughtered sheep had been buried there. That was a prize worth exhuming. They decided to let a third person in on their discovery. They actually told Burgess! Arrangements were made with him for the removal of the carcase under cover of darkness.

Burgess knew he must act swiftly. He alone must lift what was under that sod. He took up Anna and bore her away. This time she should rest in a place where, surely, no-one would ever find her.

Arrested

Burgess, who had crossed from Lynmouth to Swansea, was arrested and brought back to Simonsbath. Parson Thornton taxed him to his face to say what he had done with Anna, received no reply, and called him the very worst of murderers.

In Burgess's pocket were the boots Anna had worn when she left Mrs. Marley's house with her father. Burgess was taken to Dulverton and locked up, and the search for Anna's body continued in the Simonsbath area.

But July and August slipped by, with no result, and the Dulverton magistrates became restive. They said there was not sufficient evidence that a murder had been committed, and in the absence of a body they could not go on remanding Burgess much longer.

Then came a stroke of luck for the searchers. That man who had been skulking on the hillside on the Tuesday night after Anna's disappearance, came to Parson Thornton with a statement. He admitted he had been up to no good, but perhaps that would be overlooked if what he had to tell would help the case in hand. He had been above the Wheal Eliza mine, between it and the child's empty grave. He had heard footsteps approaching. He had seen

18

nothing, but someone had passed below him, going in a direction from the grave to the Wheal Eliza mine.

The man's tale was taken to the Dulverton magistrates and their reaction was praiseworthy. They said they would have the Wheal Eliza emptied of water and searched, and if nothing was found they would pay the bill themselves.

Tenders were invited, and the lowest, for about £350, was accepted. It took until November to clear the water from a shaft 360 feet deep. The dramatic moment had arrived. A young man volunteered to descend the rickety ladder. He was roped under the armpits for safety. At the top of the shaft a big crowd waited. When the young man came up his face had the sickly hue of shock and in his arms he carried the remains of Anna Burgess.

Shift for a Shroud

The child was parcelled in a tarpaulin coat. Inevitably, it was Parson Thornton who cut the cord. Inside was a bag. Thornton slit it. Another bag was revealed. Again Thornton cut. Only a little shift covered Anna's remains. There was nothing left of her face.

The bundle was laid in an old cottage beside the Wheal Eliza, and there Mrs. Marley swore to the hair and shift being Anna's. A coroner, three doctors, policemen and a magistrate arrived from Dulverton; the medical men made an immediate and, to Thornton, quite sickening post mortem examination. Thornton buried the remains in his churchyard.

An inquest jury sitting at Exford returned a verdict of wilful murder against Burgess and committed him to Taunton Gaol. He was tried at Somerset Assizes in the county town. When the jury returned with their verdict of guilty they were seen to be weeping!

In the condemned cell Burgess acknowledged his guilt to Thornton, said he had killed Anna because she was costing half a crown a week for lodge, and then asked that his two other children, Tom and Emma, should visit him. He particularly wished to see Emma 'as he loved her almost as much as the one he had killed'!

Thornton was taken aback by the calm way Tom and Emma received the news of their father's crime and his impending fate. They were not surprised to learn that he had done away with their sister, and they thought they were probably next on the list.

Local people said it ought to have been known all along that Anna was down the Wheal Eliza, for at night a mysterious light hovered over the shaft.

William Burgess met his end publicly on the morning of January 4th, 1859, at Taunton Gaol. He suffered, as was the saying, under Calcraft. Sometimes the phrase could be taken literally, for the lord high executioner of the day had his bungling moments.

Perhaps William Burgess did not deserve to go out too easily.

19

Postscript

Information given to the author following publication of an earlier edition of this book indicates that Burgess probably had more than murder on his conscience, and was a fire-raiser who caused the deaths of three people. Moreover, this was an incident that had a direct bearing on the subsequent fate of little Anna.

After the death of his wife Burgess tried first to place Anna with a family in the parish of Withypool. He went to a house known as South Hill and asked James Hayes and his wife Sarah to take Anna into their home. This was not convenient to them because they had a child of their own and Sarah was bearing another.

Burgess became fiendishly angry. On the night of 13th January, 1858, he took mad revenge on the South Hill family, setting fire to the house. James Hayes and his wife escaped from the blaze, but James's father, John Hayes, aged 63, and two others who were staying in the house, Matthew Shapland (22) and Grace Shapland (12) died from suffocation and burns. Their graves are in Withypool churchyard. Had Anna Burgess been received into this home she would have been safe, and three more people would have been spared a horrifying death.

I received information about this incident from Mr. Robert C. Hayes, of High Wycombe, a great-great-grandson of John Hayes, of South Hill house. It was understood in the family, said Mr. Hayes, that Burgess confessed to the arson while he lay under sentence of death. *See outside front cover for the ruins of Wheal Eliza Cottage as photographed in 1970, and page 4 as it used to be.*

5 Plug-pull for a Body

They've pulled the plug on Exmoor just twice.

The plug of the giant bath of Pinkery. Object of the exercise . . . to find a body at the bottom.

The first time, in 1889, there **was** a body. All the signs had pointed to it being there. The second time, an operation inspired entirely by assumption, the plug-pull yielded no body, but it did reveal to hundreds of people the ugly, yet awe-inspiring sight of three acres of black, moving mire in the bottom of the Pinkery basin. A spectacle never seen before and unlikely to be looked upon again.

The second plug-pull, in 1913, ranks as an epic, albeit a mucky one, of endeavour on the part of a handful of men. To pull that recalcitrant plug became a challenge subordinating the root purpose of the operation. The men of 1913 completed what their predecessors of 1889 partially achieved . . . the entire draining of Pinkery. It was all for nothing, but the satisfaction of beating a challenge was theirs.

Pinkery Pond broods its own mystery where it sits . . . a cold sheet in the boggiest, most unfrequented part of Exmoor, companion to The Chains. Hardly does it need to have brought to it the mystery of men's disappearances; it seems one with the mind's melancholia.

Apart from its alliterative chime, pond is hardly the word for Pinkery. The lake, creation of that great pioneer of Exmoor reclamation, John Knight, covers some three acres, and at 1,500 feet is the highest sheet of water in England south of the Pennine reservoirs. Knight imported 200 pick and shovel Irish navvies for the excavation in the early years of the 19th century. Only once since has the loneliness of Exmoor's most forbidding territory been invaded by a greater number of people. That was on a winter Sunday in 1913 when 250 sightseers arrived to stare at the black morass after Pinkery had been drained in the hope of finding the missing William Stenner, an Exford labourer.

Disappointed Suitor

The group of men who made their way to Pinkery in March, 1889, were hoping to recover the body of Farmer Gammon, of Bowley Barton, Parracombe, and they were sure they had come to the right place. Gammon's pony had been found tied up near the pond, and the farmer's clothes were on the bank.

Gammon, a widower of 50, had been paying persistent addresses to a young woman in the neighbourhood. Finally, she told him nicely but firmly that she did not wish to marry him and that it was useless for him to continue his advances. Gammon was heard to exclaim: 'Then I'm off to Pinkery'.

So there was little or no mystery in his disappearance, though it led to the first Pinkery plug-pull. First, the pond was dragged, and a Cardiff diver went down several times. It was then decided to empty the pond by withdrawing one of the two great plugs in the double drain pipes, an operation entrusted to Messrs. Jones Bros., of Lynton. Only partial draining was necessary before the farmer's body was discovered.

Different Story

The second plug-pull, in 1913, was a very different story. This time there had been a most unaccountable disappearance. William Stenner, aged 41, married, with six children, had not been seen since he left his home at Riscombe, near White Cross, Exford, on the evening of August 9th, 1912. He had been complaining of sleeplessness, but apparently had no other worries. He went to bed early on August 9th. His wife looked in on him to say she was going to make him a cup of tea, and when she came up again the bed was empty. Stenner could not have left the house in the normal way without being seen, and it was established later that he had made his exit through the bedroom window.

The scope of the search for Stenner was commensurate with that for Mollie Phillips, the Exford girl, in 1929. Practically every

Pinkery Pond drained in 1913, showing the well, the plug and the 12-inch pipe.

able-bodied man and youth in Exford and Withypool volunteered. They were led by two men with an intimate knowledge of the moor—Morland Greig, Master of the Devon and Somerset Stag-hounds, and Yalden Thompson, Master of the Exmoor Foxhounds.

In January of the following year, probably in recollection that Pinkery Pond had yielded the body of Gammon, it was decided to attempt a plug-pull on chance of finding Stenner. One wonders why the worst month of winter was chosen for such an operation in the bleakest area of Exmoor. The moor was mantled in snow, and many wet days followed. It goes to show the dogged spirit that possessed men. The searchers were giving freely of their time without the slightest prospect of reward, and they were tackling Pinkery on pure assumption, there being not the slightest clue that the missing man may have gone there.

Of the horde of volunteers who had engaged in the original search for Stenner, there remained a small but doughty band for the Pinkery plug-pull. In the last days of the endeavour the number was down to five, and the crowning moments of success . . . one might almost call them the 'moments of truth' . . . were shared by three men only.

The extraction of the Pinkery plug, which changed three acres of bright water into a deep chasm of black ooze, proved an engineering feat lasting four weeks.

Claustrophobic

Although the operation has always been popularly termed the Pinkery plug-pull, as if a giant hand had to pull a chain releasing a plug from a bath hole, it was really a plug-**push**. There were two huge plugs, shaped like a cork, rimmed, and made of English oak. They were, of course, on the pond side of the dam wall, and each fitted into an iron pipe nine feet long. The pipes, one above the other, were approached by a tunnel 60 yards long and less than three feet high in places, and it was in this claustrophobic confine that the last three men on the job had to work.

In spite of the weather's apparent designs that the task should not succeed, the men were within an ace of triumph by January 28th. They had partially forced the plug of the higher pipe, and the pond had practically run out, but by some means the plug re-blocked the pipe, the flow of water stopped, and the level rose very quickly. Indeed, it became higher than it had been before the plug was touched!

Had four weeks' toil been wasted? 'Not on your life', was the reaction of Mr. J. Kingdon, of Driver Farm, the leading spirit in the operation. He was determined on a complete draining of Pinkery; that, and that alone, would show whether or not William Stenner's body was there. If it was, then it was likely to be near the pipe under the wall of the dam, where there was also an artificial well 10 to 15 feet deep. This well had been "felt for" with poles.

The well and the slopes above it must be completely drained to make the finished job. And curiosity had been growing . . . to see how the drainage system worked.

Two men, Wensley and Kivell, who had been working zealously with Kingdon, were not available when on Wednesday night the last-named set out from Driver Farm with lamps, and the last act was shared by Kingdon and two others, H. F. Tudball, of Ashnott, and Alfred Vowles, of Minehead.

The lamps were lighted, and Kingdon led the way into the long tunnel. To push the plug out into the pond an enormous iron bar, 29 feet long and weighing seven cwt., was put into the pipe. 'One, two three . . . ram'.

Tunnel Fright

A terrific roar came from the pipe, the plug yielded, and black water gushed around the feet of the men in the tunnel. But the volume did not satisfy Kingdon. The bar was withdrawn, the plug re-seated itself, and the flow stopped. Eight times more the men rammed the bar against the plug, and then it was decided to force it open still more by using an hydraulic jack. This weighed 140lbs. and was capable of lifting 20 tons. It was placed against the end of the bar on a raised platform.

Kingdon was doing the technical work, Tudball paddled up and down the winding tunnel fetching gear, and Vowles was the lamp man. Later, he described his role as 'keeping still, getting wet, and looking on like a frightened cat'.

And fright there was. The jack forced the plug so far that a tremendous rush of water came through, but suddenly the gear and its supporting platform collapsed, and for a moment all was chaos in the tunnel. The men were lucky to escape injury. Their chief concern was that the plug had slipped back into the pipe, again completely stopping the flow of water.

All the labour had to start again. 'Never mind, us'll win yet', said Kingdon. Victory came at 7 o'clock, the tunnel roared with the surge of water, and the men beat a retreat.

Falling and Rolling

Lamp bearer Vowles described for the *West Somerset Free Press* his feelings on exchanging the foul atmosphere of the tunnel for the piercing keenness of the open air on a January night on the moor. 'I seemed unable to stand upright or walk straight. I had three or four falls and rolls after leaving the tunnel, and it was five minutes before I gained my equilibrium. Soaked to the skin and covered with mud from head to foot, we fought our way back to Driver Farm, rolling some of the way, falling and slipping over some of the roughest country. We all had falls across Hundred Acres, but the humour of the exciting situation was splendid'!

They were back at Pinkery at 9 a.m. on Thursday. They found the pond almost out of water but, ominously, an area under the dam wall was submerged, and the height of the water was increasing. The pipe had become blocked again!

Back into the tunnel . . . more ramming, more blockings, until at 1 p.m. a great roar was heard in the well, water and mud disappeared and pipe and plug were revealed. For the first time since Pinkery was built 100 years before, its bed was uncovered.

Kingdon's last act was to pull the plug up from its black bed and lay it on firm ground. Perhaps he suitably addressed the plug, but of this there is no record!

There is a steep descent to the well from the main pond. The stream flowing through the bed moved masses of liquid mud, and a drained Pinkery registered an impression of a huge black morass moving slowly towards the dam wall.

The pond was seen in this state by about 250 people, most of whom came on one day. Two weeks later the plugs were restored and Pinkery became once more a lake. But the mystery of William Stenner remained.

Close to Home

In the last week of February Stenner's body was found . . . no more than 400 yards from his cottage at Riscombe!

After the toilers' epic of draining a three-acre lake miles away, it must have been ironic to learn that Stenner was lying in a small chamber of water behind a rock, and accessible through a hole only two feet wide. In fact, the entrance would compare unfavourably in size with many a badger earth.

And a further irony . . . this very place had been the first searched after Stenner's disappearance. It was known as Muddicombe, reached after a climb of 400 yards from Stenner's cottage along the road to White Post. Here stood the ruins of a house and outbuildings. In a rocky bank was a hole through which Stenner had squeezed himself, to dive to his self-drowning in a waterlogged chamber behind the rock. This was really the site of an adit driven many years previously when mining was the industrial vogue on Exmoor. The shaft ran downwards at first, and then up into a coppice.

The body was located through the keen perception of a farm worker, Reginald Hookway, who had gone to Muddicombe to tend cattle. The small hole in the rock intrigued him; he peered in and thought he could see something white.

Hookway fetched a hay fork, prodded . . . and the missing man mystery was solved.

Although Stenner contributed to the epic plug-pull of Pinkery, it seems remarkable that the search was ever concentrated so far from his home. For when he left his cottage on the evening of August 9, 1912, he was clad only in his shirt. Severe rain was lashing the hills, and in these conditions and his own it was unlikely that the poor man could have survived the night or wandered very far.

6 With Malice Aforethought

A cartridge for a shotgun may contain 130 to 140 shots.

And a man whose right lung has been blasted with 117 of them has but a short time to live.

Henry Pugsley staggered indoors to die.

The man who had shot him walked calmly into his own house and upstairs . . . to finish himself.

But Henry Quartly, expert handler of the double-barrel, who had just blasted his neighbour to death in the street at a range of 36 feet, missed himself with his second shot.

Now he would have to meet the hangman.

There had been bad blood in the street. Now, to the horror of the village in the vale, the figurative had become the life-draining literal.

The blood in the street was real. It lay where the wounded man had clutched the railings of his house for support.

Murder in Porlock . . . almost in the western style. A man shot in the back. The murder weapon aimed from behind a garden wall topped by bushes and bright flowers.

A killing without mystery as far as the physical act was concerned. Henry Quartly had blasted his double-barrel shotgun into Henry Pugsley's back.

But surely there was something behind the shot, behind the steady aim, the nerveless trigger-finger?

Swooning Girl

Henry Quartly had reckoned so coolly when he lined up his victim. He had not anticipated that a shot would splay off and hit an 18-year-old girl in the chest. He was upset that this should have happened. Alice Middleton was not seriously wounded, but she swooned and fell to the ground, and for a few minutes Porlock people thought they had witnessed a double tragedy.

Alice had been talking in Parson Street with Mrs. Chapman, a neighbour of Henry Pugsley, and his wife, Fanny. At that moment the neighbourliness of a village street was shattered by a man with a gun. He, too, had been a neighbour, and a decent one . . . up to the time of a change in his attitude the previous year. It was a change toward the Pugsleys, no-one else.

Henry Quartly, preparing for the suicide he bungled, had stuffed a note into his pocket: 'I got no grievance against no-one else, only those two Pugsleys'.

It was Wednesday, June 3, 1914, when Henry Quartly ended the life of his neighbour. We must put back the clock to December 3, 1913.

Case Dismissed

The magistrates in the old court-house at Dunster, by the side of the A.39, had had a longish sit on December 3. There was a case of a man failing to stamp insurance cards for his employees; another, which was contested, of an hotel landlord being found drunk on licensed premises.

These cases ran to more than two columns of space in the local newspaper. A great deal less had been devoted to a third case before the magistrates. The proceedings were short, and no clear background picture emerges.

Henry Quartly (55), mason, of Parson Street, Porlock, was summoned for using indecent language within the hearing of the highway at Porlock on October 31st, 1913. He did not admit the charge.

The complainant was Mrs. Fanny Pugsley, of Parson Street. She said she had been tenant of her house for 32 years. She and her husband, Henry, were fruiterers and fish dealers. She complained that Quartly had entered her house and used disgraceful language.

Quartly denied using the language alleged. He said Mrs. Pugsley had been interfering with a tenant, Thomas Heard, who had complained about it to him (Quartly). It was not the first time Heard had complained to him.

That was all there was to the case. The magistrates dismissed it 'for want of sufficient evidence to convict'.

Had they convicted, the Porlock murder in the following year might have been prevented. A conviction might have brought Quartly up sharply. Something was rankling with him. Up to now he had been a friendly type. The villagers said he was brooding on the court case.

Whatever the shadow that had come between Quartly and the Pugsleys, it led to another summons, of the same kind as before. Quartly was due to answer it at the Dunster court on June 5th, 1914.

Instead, he would be at the court on the capital charge of murder.

Tragedy at Tea-time

The Hawkcombe Valley funnels into Porlock through the confine of Parson Street, opening out by the parish church into the main street.

Henry Pugsley, who was 59, lived in a low, old-fashioned house, fronted with trellis railings, opposite the Victoria Reading Room in Parson Street. On the other side, beyond the entrance to Rectory Field, was Henry Quartly's house. Quartly had a garden on the same side of the road as Pugsley's home, and some 12½ yards from it. That was the distance of the shooting.

Just before six o'clock on June 3 Henry Pugsley and his wife returned in their pony and trap from a business round on Exmoor. Brendon had been their last place of call. A cup of tea was indicated, and Mrs. Pugsley put the kettle on while her husband made the pony snug in a stable a little way from his house.

Pugsley started to walk to his house. He passed Quartly's garden,

27

had a word with Mrs. Chapman, who was in the street . . . then it happened.

A gunshot from Quartly's garden, from behind the bushes and bright flowers topping a 4 feet 6 inches high wall.

Marmion Watts had just turned into Parson Street with his horse and cart and had come abreast of Pugsley's house. John Bass was bringing his cart from the direction of the Rectory garden. Mrs. Chapman and Alice Middleton were there.

It was tea-time for George Bushen and his wife, Kitty. The report of a shot rattled through their cottage and they went to the door.

Both caught a glimpse of Henry Quartly behind the bushes in his garden. A gun was at his shoulder. Alice Middleton lay prone in the street, and Henry Pugsley was slumping against his railings, holding his back. Marmion Watts' horse was rearing and plunging.

Mrs. Pugsley came out to her stricken husband. 'I'm shot, mother', was all he said. Indoors, his life ebbing fast, he did not speak again.

'My husband would never have given an angry word to anyone', wept Mrs. Pugsley. 'He was beloved in Porlock'.

Constable's Tackle

Joseph Greedy was Porlock's police constable, the solid, dependable bobby of the beat.

He was off duty and in plain clothes when someone ran to fetch him. He did not bother to change into uniform. He grabbed his handcuffs, and ran. He knew intuitively that he was setting out to make an arrest.

As he approached the scene he saw the fallen figure of Alice Middleton. He also saw Mrs. Pugsley helping her husband indoors, and she called out to Greedy, 'Look what Quartly has done to my husband'.

But Greedy's attention was diverted from the Pugsleys and Alice Middleton by the sound of a shot coming from Quartly's house. Greedy hurried in, paused at a muttering of voices, and then went quietly up the stairs. He found Quartly's sister, Emily, pacing to and fro in a bedroom. She was startled to see him, but immediately warned him with a 'Look out, Mr. Greedy, else he will shoot you too'.

But Joseph Greedy saw his duty and went to it. In a curtained recess stood Quartly, holding his gun. In a flash Greedy sprang. He knocked the gun from Quartly's hand, threw him on his back on the floor and shouted for help. Up the stairs came Robert Huish and a man named Blackmore.

The handcuffs clicked, and Henry Quartly would never be a free man again. He had come so close to putting an end to himself. His face bore traces of powder, there was blood on his lip, and a shot-hole in the ceiling.

Greedy lost no time in conveying Quartly to Dunster police station, the local police H.Q., presided over by Supt. Perry. Greedy had his prisoner, but without knowing quite what he had got him for. He had gone off without checking on Pugsley's fate; he did not know that the shot man died within a few minutes of getting indoors. And Greedy was also remembering Alice Middleton lying in the road.

So it was that Quartly was originally charged at Dunster with shooting with intent to kill. Indeed, Greedy first mentioned Alice Middleton. Quartly replied that he had had no intention of harming her; it was 'Tacker' Pugsley he had been after. 'Tacker' was Pugsley's nickname.

Straight Admission

When Pugsley was mentioned Quartly made a reply typical of his attitude for the remainder of his time. Indeed, it could not be otherwise. 'I shot him, that is straight, that is the truth, so there is an end of it'.

Perry immediately drove to Porlock, found a dead man, and returned to Dunster to charge Quartly with murder. Quartly again admitted the shooting . . . and asked how long Pugsley had taken to die.

Quartly was removed to Exeter gaol. Told he could attend the inquest on Pugsley if he wished, he said there was no point in him being there.

The inquest, held at the Victoria Reading Room, a few yards from the scene of the shooting, was, in the fashion of the times, more like trial proceedings than a mere inquiry into 'how and by what means Henry Pugsley came to his death'. The evidence given matched exactly that heard later by the Dunster magistrates when they committed Quartly to stand trial at the next Somerset Assize.

At the inquest P.C. Greedy heard himself commended. Said the coroner: 'The police in country villages sometimes have a rough time'.

The jury's verdict was that Henry Quartly did feloniously, wilfully and with malice aforethought murder Henry Pugsley.

Guinea Reward

Supt. Perry announced that the Chief Constable of Somerset had instructed him to give Robert Huish a guinea in token of his valued assistance to P.C. Greedy in overpowering Quartly.

Henry Pugsley passed through Porlock on a wheeled bier to his funeral service in the Wesleyan church, where the Rev. Jabez Wright spoke of him as 'a kind, industrious, genial man'.

Tributes could also have been paid to Quartly . . . at one time. There was the tragedy. The killer and the killed . . . both had been respected and both had many friends.

29

Quartly was a strong, sporting type; cricketer, footballer, a notably staunch defender in the latter game. And he had been the reverse of morose. On the morning of the murder he had gone to the Royal Oak Inn for a drink, and Landlord James Lamb said later in court that he was 'jolly and joking with the customers, just as he always did'.

Murder is 'the crime apart'. After six o'clock on that Wednesday evening, the previous character of Henry Quartly had ceased to matter.

Keeping it Short

Wearisome processes of the law were not for Henry Quartly.

He was arraigned at Somerset Assize at Wells on October 20, before Mr. Justice Atkin.

The proceedings were only a formality . . . and Quartly was determined to keep them that way. They lasted precisely nine minutes.

But in that short time a lot was said in trying to delay the inevitable. It irritated the man who was quite ready to take what was coming to him.

Quartly insisted on pleading guilty and could not understand how it could possibly be suggested that he should make the opposite plea.

In gaol at Shepton Mallet he had refused to see Freddy Willmott, the Taunton solicitor who had represented him at the magistrates court proceedings at Dunster. And he forbade Willmott to instruct counsel to appear at the Assize. Willmott, however, contacted counsel, and W. H. Duckworth came down from London to represent Quartly. But Quartly refused to have anything to do with him.

The situation was explained to Mr. Justice Atkin, and Duckworth asked him if he would allow Quartly's guilty plea to be withdrawn so that the case could be proved. Duckworth thought this desirable in view of Quartly's attitude.

Mr. Justice Atkin told Duckworth: 'I don't see, if you are not appearing for the accused, what you can do'.

Duckworth agreed he could do nothing unless the plea of guilty was withdrawn and the judge authorised him to act for Quartly.

To this the judge replied: 'I can't authorise you to act for him if he is not willing to have you'.

'An end to it'

The judge then told Quartly that he was not obliged to plead guilty, but Quartly burst out: 'I know I am guilty. What's the use of bamboozling about it? What's the use to go over it all again? I killed him, and there's an end to it'.

The judge tried again. 'Quartly', he said, 'the question is whether the whole of the facts ought not to be proved and inquiry made as to your condition when you shot Pugsley. I think you had better plead not guilty'.

'I say guilty', responded Quartly. 'I don't want to squeeze out of it'.

Still Mr. Justice Atkin tried. 'It seems to me that it may not be a proper verdict to say 'Wilful Murder',' he commented.

Duckworth was also trying. He said the judge would have known cases where, notwithstanding the desire of the prisoner, a plea had been withdrawn and another substituted.

'It doesn't seem to me that there is any necessity to do so in this case', said the judge. 'The man knows what he is about'.

So all efforts to persuade Quartly to accept counsel failed, and he was asked if he had anything further to say why sentence should not now be passed.

From his pocket Quartly drew a slip of paper and began to read. 'I shot him and I must expect to be killed. I can only die once. I fear no foe. I am leaving my old friends behind me, but I hope to meet them all some day. I hope they will cheer up and keep up their pecker'.

The black cap was now upon Mr. Justice Atkin's head. He addressed Quartly. 'You have pleaded guilty in circumstances which make it quite plain that you knew what you were doing. You shot this man almost, as it were, in the presence of his wife'.

Quartly cut the judge off in the midst of his stride. 'I wish I had shot *her*, too', he exclaimed. The papers have a phrase for such interjections . . . Sensation in court.

Mr. Justice Atkin's voice was now very cold. 'You seem to be full of spite against the woman you deprived of her husband',he said.

Then he pronounced sentence of death.

Quartly turned to go below. 'Well, goodbye all', he shouted.

Eight O'clock Walk

Henry Quartly met the hangman at 8 a.m. on Tuesday, November 10. It was Thomas W. Pierrepoint, a name not unknown in business connected with the science of the drop.

Pierrepoint, operating without an assistant, carried out his duty most expeditiously. So said the newspapers. On such occasions they liked to be comforting and to pay tribute where it was due. They stood in no danger of contradiction.

Quartly was the fourth person to be hanged at Shepton Mallet. Since the previous execution a new gallows and execution house had been erected near the centre of the gaol and close to the condemned cell. This obviated a procession which on former hanging occasions had had to pass points within view of the public.

The ghouls who gathered outside the gaol were denied the thrill of 'the moment of truth' . . . the noise of the drop. Under the 'new arrangement' it was too far away to be heard.

P.C. Joseph Greedy's bravery in tackling an armed man was marked by the award to him of the King's police medal.

31

7 Sudden Departure

Mystery . . . or merely the mouth of mischief?

Count Conrad Hochberg, a German nobleman with an English home, had vanished from it.

His home was the mansion of Croydon Hall, nestling in a secluded dell at the top of a hill reached by several lanes leading off south from the A.39 road between Washford and Minehead.

It was not, as wild newspaper reports sought to show, 'perched on a headland in an almost inaccessible corner of Exmoor, 1,500 feet above the channel waves'.

That was the trouble. Exmoor has its cloak and dagger . . . the swirling mist and the cutting wind, and from the moment Count Hochberg disappeared from 'his domain on the eve of the 1914-18 war the imaginations were busy in creating out of whispers on the wind the cloak and dagger elements of espionage.

It reads like vintage melodrama, at times not far removed from the pages of a schoolboy's adventure paper. But war had come, and the word German was suddenly a dirty one.

Local spymania ran riot on the tongue and in the Press. It ran just about as far as it could breathlessly go . . . even to a story that the German Emperor himself, Kaiser Wilhelm, had visited Exmoor in pre-war days to meet the Count he had caused to be 'planted' here for espionage purposes.

The picture of a kind of walkie-talkie on Exmoor between the German Head of State and a henchman, is difficult to sustain, but it was created. And perhaps a story that the Kaiser came incognito, travelling to Minehead by pleasure steamer from Bristol, should be taken with more than a pinch or two of Bristol Channel salt. But stories they were.

Count Conrad Hochberg, rich and good-natured, was a member of the royal house of Pless. Often he proclaimed his love for England and its country pursuits, and the majority of local people were convinced of his sincerity. If that sincerity needed underwriting the Count would appear to have done it himself in his beneficence to the district.

Throughout the weeks of rumour that Croydon Hall's head was a spy for his Fatherland, and that the Hall was an arsenal for weapons that would be used against the people in the event of invasion, the friends of the Count subscribed to the picture he had created . . . good neighbour of the good gentry around him, kindly benefactor of deserving causes, staunch Anglican, man of horse and hound (he gave 100 guineas annually to the Devon and Somerset Staghounds), lavish entertainer, acceptable after-dinner speaker, friend of the poor, exhibitor at agricultural shows.

The Count was a cousin of the Kaiser and a Captain in the

famous White Cuirassiers at Potsdam. He was a younger brother of Prince Henry of Pless, who married a daughter of Colonel Cornwallis West, of Ruthin Castle, North Wales. Conrad had a younger brother, Count Friedrich Hochberg, who was living at Minsted Manor, in Hampshire.

On August 4th, 1914, England found herself at war with Germany, and Croydon Hall had lost its Count. Where was he?

Property Seized

On August 8, Sir Prior Goldney, a county magistrate, went to Croydon Hall, accompanied by police officers. They were armed with a warrant. The staff at the Hall were told that the Count's 21 horses were being seized on behalf of the Crown, and that a police watch would be kept on the house. Subsequently the whole property and its contents were seized.

The national Press fed richly on rumour. Thin it might be, but it was easy to stuff it out. Stories suggested that the Hall had been a spy centre for years. The local weekly newspapers, sober reflectors of the life of the district, and loyal to it, poured ineffectual scorn upon the popular daily press and expressed the indignation of local people that a generous gentleman was being baselessly maligned.

A statement appeared in a daily that on the morning war was declared the Count told his staff they might never see him again . . . 'and disappeared'.

'Where'? asked the Rector of Old Cleeve, the Rev. G. Weigall, with a cutting edge to his question. 'Down a trap-door, or in a blue flame'?

Old Cleeve was the Count's parish, and it was in the Rector's church that he had served as a churchwarden and lesson reader. And on a bench-end his coat-of-arms had been carved.

Last Garden Party

Hochberg had come to Croydon Hall in 1907; he left it, never to return, on July 28th, 1914, seven days before the declaration of war between England and Germany. The date of his departure was later verified. It disposes of the rumour that he said goodbye to his staff on August 4 and 'just disappeared'.

It must be granted that a man of Hochberg's standing and intelligence would have appreciated the fateful trend of European events that summer.

Or was it a case of intelligence, in a sinister sense, having been received . . . or even brought to the Count by the Kaiser himself, voyaging to Minehead on that pleasure steamer? In days to come people would whisper that it was.

The worsening international situation had made no difference to the West Somerset social round. As late as July 24th Hochberg gave a big garden party at Croydon Hall for a large number of

Croydon Hall

guests. They came in 45 motor cars and 15 carriages. Hochberg must have known it was his farewell to the English friends he had been cultivating for the past seven years, though he would not be telling them so. As usual, he played the part of the generous and affable host to perfection. He may not have said goodbye to his friends, but he did to his flowers. His gardens were magnificent. Now he went around gently touching his English roses, here and there stopping to inhale their scent or to snip off a dead bud.

Hochberg made one personal farewell. That was to the Rector of Old Cleeve, whom he told that he was volunteering for service in Germany in the Red Cross. Later, that statement was to be used by the Count's friends as testimony to his good faith. Here, they said, was a man who so loved England that he would not fight against her but would engage in humanitarian work.

'Blow up the Hall'

Hochberg reached London with the spy rumours at his heels. One newspaper account suggested darkly that in making plans for quitting England Hochberg was far in advance of the rest of the German gentry then living in this country.

The same account had it that on August 3rd Hochberg was found at Folkestone, trying to obtain a passage across the channel, and was arrested by officials. He was, said this account, taken to London, where he obtained an interview with the Ambassador, who placed him at the head of a German party for whom he had secured a passport. The Ambassador held that Hochberg was not of military qualification. To honour this decision, Hochberg did not re-enter the German Army or fight in the war. He accepted high office in the Red Cross.

Another account had Hochberg trying to leave the country by Dover, 'where he was arrested as a spy'.

If that was so, then one ought to have him making a defiant gesture, if not a bid for freedom. We were not disappointed. The account said that Hochberg managed to send a wire to a servant at Croydon Hall, ordering him to blow up the premises and its secret arsenal.

Just the stuff for the schoolboy. But with Croydon Hall remaining secure on its foundations, we had to be told why. And here it was. The servant had been disobedient of his master's command. He had taken the wire to the police.

The wild pens were taking wings in constructing a sinister picture of the Count. The physical description applied to him was a stock one that would have done for any novel of the times requiring a villain. He was 'a tall man of military apparance, clean shaven, with sallow features and a saturnine expression'. He just had to be! It was a little too early for a Clubfoot, but the writers might have given the Count a limp for good value.

The Count, we were told, spent £60,000 on building his stronghold 'on the cliffs'. The nearest cliff to Croydon Hall is about six miles away!

Now to the stronghold itself. It was built to 'extraordinary plans'. From every window the inmates 'could observe the shipping in the Bristol Channel'. And 'an approaching stranger was within view long before he reached the door of the Hall'.

'The Hall was lit by electricity generated on the estate' (which a man as wealthy as the Count could easily afford). The very mention of light seemed to leave the occupants of the Hall in sinister shadow. The hum of a generator must imply the wicked machination of a presiding mind.

'Rifles Galore'

As for the story of the Count ordering his servant to blow up the Hall, there had to be something to warrant such a dire command. So we must not be surprised to read of 'a cache of 300 rifles, a Marconi radio set, storage tanks containing 7,000 gallons of petrol, incriminating documents and the plans of the coast and defences around Minehead'.

A comment that the Court's water supply came from a well ninety feet deep is a carefully selected expression. No doubt we were intended to associate the well with the depth of intrigue at the Hall.

The actual findings by the police on their visit to the 'inaccessible stronghold' make dull reading . . . a pair of twelve-bore guns, a rabbit rifle, 211 cartridges loaded with No. 6 shot'!

'Almost exactly what you would find at any time in *my* house', said the first Lord St. Audries. He was writing to Colonel Cornwallis West, commiserating with him over the distress the Hochberg stories were causing. The Count was a brother-in-law of the Colonel's daughter, Princess Pless.

The petrol found at the Hall amounted to 800 gallons, not an excessive amount when it is considered that the Count kept four powerful motor cars and that filling stations in villages were practically unknown.

Pleadings

Croydon Hall, bereft of its owner, remained ringed with his friends.

In a letter to the Press the Rev. C. H. Shaw, vicar of the adjoining parish of Leighland, declared: 'There is nothing about the Count's movements or his house that can give rise to the slightest suspicion that he has been anything but a straightforward and honourable gentleman'.

Another writer pleaded: 'Spare a feeling for one who in the dread necessity of war has had to leave the English home he has loved'.

And the rector of Old Cleeve: 'If it is proved that the gentleman was preparing the way for a German invasion and yet was kept so uninformed of the intentions of his own government that he had the greatest difficulty in reaching his own country when war broke out, we have not much to fear from the German Intelligence Department'.

The Count was now in Germany, and the warring nations went about their business. The spy rumours died for duration.

Here They Come Again

Ten years after the war there was a grand resurrection of the Hochberg stories. Fiction again tussled with fact . . . and scored heavily.

Croydon Hall was now re-sited . . . in Devon! We read that 'the Count was receiving German guests in his well-constructed mansion. He made one very large room shut off from the others except by a passage'.

So, after ten years, someone introduces the jolly old passage, without which no thriller of those days would have been complete. There was much more for entertainment. 'The walls of the room were padded, so as to shut in all sounds. The doors were double, and the steel windows were heavily shuttered and the crevices packed. Cupboards all round the room were locked, and it was afterwards revealed that they contained rifles and ammunition. Outside the house were several emplacements for large guns, which looked right out over the Severn Sea, and near each emplacement was an underground magazine for ammunition'.

The re-hashed stories had the Kaiser visiting the Hall in pre-war days. The Count's car had met him at Minehead, where he disembarked from a pleasure steamer, and was whisked away to the stronghold.

And the final banality: 'Hochberg kept exceedingly close to his visitor. They breakfasted alone and occupied adjoining bedrooms. After breakfast they generally set off for a long walk, lasting all day, each carrying a sporting rifle, and they paid particular attention to the emplacements for guns'.

Purged

The last local act in the Hochberg story was performed in Old Cleeve church.

It was 1918. Four years of war, of colossal casualties that touched even the smallest rural communities with the chill of death, had stirred up the bitterness and the hate. The only good German was a dead one . . . and Count Hochberg was presumed to be alive. No longer had he champions in the district; certainly none willing to be vocal on his behalf. If they still saw him as the likeable country squire, it was not prudent to say so. And even if he had not been this country's enemy he was culpable at root . . . he was a German.

And so the parishioners of Old Cleeve, in vestry assembled, decided to apply to the Diocesan Chancellor for a faculty wherewith to purge a church bench-end of an alien and enemy device, to wit, the Count's coat-of-arms.

The pathetic little job was carried out with the minimum publicity.

No evidence was ever uncovered that Hochberg had been a spy for the Kaiser.

Talk with aged people who remember the Count, and they say they suppose there *must* have been 'something funny going on at the Hall'. Press them, and they can point to nothing. It is all in the mind. The seeds of mischief planted nearly sixty years ago brought forth but a weakly fruit of mystery, but the seeds may linger until the last person who remembers the Count has passed on.

When Hochberg died he was buried in a Berlin cemetery. His funeral service was that of the Church of England, only English hymns were sung, and a sermon in English was preached.

If this was not a bluff, then Count Hochberg had given his detractors their answer from his coffin.

The Count's Monogram at Croydon Hall today.

8 The Footsteps of Fear

The breastplate on the coffin was inscribed: 'Gwendoline Mollie Phillips, died 8th September, 1929, aged 17 years".

Died. But how? And why? And who could say with certainty, where?

It was 2 p.m. on Sunday, September 8, 1929. Mollie Phillips (her second name was invariably used) called out as she left Rocks Farm, in the parish of Exford: 'Don't worry about the chickens. I shall be back before dark'.

She was not. Nor did she ever return. Around her spun the Exmoor mystery that lacks a completely satisfying explanation, and over which so many people shook their heads and muttered darkly.

This was the disappearance case that had everything . . . nation-wide publicity, a search of fifty square miles of Exmoor, questions in Parliament, a statement by the Attorney General, dark suspicions, theories by the score, a parson stirring things up from his pulpit, an inquest verdict which legal minds held to be inconsistent.

Add rumours wild to the point of stupidity, others nasty to the point of hurt, so that a farmer demanded that the police should specially search his house to convince people that the missing girl's body was not there.

Throw in debates on Exmoor bogs and what they could or could not do to man and beast . . . stories of floundering horses, counter-stories of heavy men weight-testing a bog and finding no danger.

All these were facets of the Mollie Phillips mystery.

Groping Through The Mist

Mollie Phillips had gone out into the bright, hot September afternoon and had vanished into thin air. The proverbial expression seemed the only one through which local people could express their bewilderment. It was as if a thick Exmoor mist had settled in perpetuity, a mist through which the police were trying to grope, on and off, for the next eighteen months, occasionally seeing a sliver of light, which quickly closed over, leaving the mist unbroken and the police stubbing toes against dead ends.

September slid sunnily away, October made autumn, Exmoor's visitors went home, and the winds moaned cold over a moorland that might be keeping a secret.

Supt. D. Hallett, in charge of the Dunster police division, was eighteen months from his retirement. No officer who had reached that anticipatory stage ever had less time to think about his future in slippers than had Hallett. He was never going to forget his last eighteen months in the force.

Sturdy, healthy, happy, with no noticeable interest in the opposite sex . . . that was the common word picture of Mollie Phillips. Everyone spoke highly of her. She worked at Rocks Farm for Mr. Leslie Tucker, and her home was about a mile away at Rocks Cottage. She was one of two daughters of Mrs. Henrietta Ford, by the latter's first marriage.

On the afternoon Mollie left Rocks Farm she was wearing a blue dress. A blue tammy fitted snugly over her dark hair. She wore tortoishell-rimmed glasses and carried a lightweight coat. She had the afternoon and evening off from work, and it was her declared intention to go to Cutcombe to visit her aunt, Mrs. White. She did not arrive there.

At Rocks Farm Mollie had called her goodbye and made her remark about being back before dark to Annie Rawle, the housekeeper. She also said she was going to find out if Tommy Heard's bus was running that day; if not, she would walk to Cutcombe.

To get the bus, Mollie would have had to walk from Rocks Farm about a quarter of a mile across a field, to strike the main road at a place called Round Water. The bus, in fact, was not operating that day.

The moment the girl left the farmhouse she would be out of sight to anybody there. She must have walked . . . somewhere. Distance and direction will never be known. She walked out of Exford's life . . . out of her own.

Hunt

A great hunt of the moorland was organised. It grew in strength and scope as the days went by. Big volunteer parties, with the Crown Hotel at Exford as a base, assisted the police. In the heart of the hunting country many horsemen were available. The splendid troop of cavalry was supported by infantry, local men who included strong swimmers capable of entering disused mine shafts. A pond near Rocks Farm was emptied, ditches were searched, moorland, fields and woods combed, and eventually there was coverage of fifty square miles of Exmoor. The quest spread westward nearly into Challacombe, then eastward, jumping from Exmoor to the Brendon Hills and into the Luxborough area, where the girl's parents lived before coming to Exford. Nothing remotely resembling a lead was found.

Fifteen months passed. It was 1931 and the year had run into spring.

Secret Of The Bog

Old man Dunkery had known all along the answer to the Mollie Phillips affair.

The lofty crown of Exmoor is silent keeper of sights and sounds . . . strolling lovers, happy picknickers, stealthily moving stags.

Search party for Mollie Phillips starting out from Exford, 1929.

It must have seen what happened on Codsend Moor . . . murder, manslaughter, or just misadventure. But the secret is locked for ever as the seasons spread their changing garments across the hill.

Codsend Moor is about 150 acres in extent. On the afternoon of Friday, March 27th, Donald Grant, tenant of Hawkington Farm, in Cutcombe parish, was on Codsend with his man, Jack Hawkins. They were burning up rough grass.

Search parties had covered Codsend Moor in the autumn of 1929 and had found nothing. Now, in the centre of the moor, about a mile from Higherhouse Farm, and 160 paces from a track leading up to Dunkery, Grant found himself staring at a bleached human skull and the bones of the right side of a person's chest.

The hunt for Mollie Phillips was over.

The bones were protruding from a spring of water in boggy ground. A few fragments of clothing could be seen nearby.

The body was in line with a hunting gate on one side of an allotment and a gate on the other. A direct line for a walker . . . or someone running . . . away from someone else?

Why should Mollie Phillips have been on Codsend Moor at all? It was well out of her way if she was going from Rocks Farm to Cutcombe.

It was not feasible to try to extricate the remains from the bog on the day of the finding. Throughout Friday night a policeman kept watch at the spot. A night on Codsend Moor! It must have been one of the eeriest vigils in the annals of tragedy.

The police sent for the Somerset Spilsbury, Dr. Godfrey Carter. On Saturday the veteran pathologist walked, with Supt. Hallett and other police officers, from Dunkery Hill Gate, two miles to where the remains lay.

A walk, in Carter's own words, 'across rough, trackless moor, where bogs and running water were encountered, and where the ground near the body was very treacherous'.

And Exmoor was about to become a debating chamber for the people. The subject . . . are the bogs really dangerous?

Donald Grant had become the tenant of Hawkington Farm in 1930, six months after Mollie Phillips disappeared. He described the place where she was found as more of a spring than a bog, and he knew of no accident to stock there.

It was his opinion that if the girl had been walking from gate to gate across the moor and had fallen into the boggy patch she would not be likely to get sucked down.

But Jack Hawkins, who had been three years at Hawkington, knew the bog as 'dangerous'. Anyone getting in would have difficulty in getting out, he said at the inquest on Mollie Phillips. He also said that six horses and nearly fifty bullocks had been grazing in the vicinity of the bog at the time the girl disappeared.

The summer of 1929 had been dry. And in September the bog

would have been dry, said Hawkins. Yet he added that it would still be dangerous.

Rabbit-trapper Jack Pugsley knew Codsend and this particular place well. 'Very deceiving', he called it. He had been in 'as deep as his thigh'. This bog was 'one of the worst places on Exmoor'. He had seen sheep in there with only their backs and heads above surface.

The Surface Shook

We will return to the police party and Dr. Carter as they approach the place. Carter notes it as 'a watery bog'. The party are three or four yards from the body and cannot get closer. Carter probes around him with his walking stick and can find no bottom anywhere.

He and the police officers shake themselves. Even that causes the surface around them to move.

The body is on its left side, above the level of the black, peaty water. Now to recover it. Deep trenches are dug to drain away the water and are then filled with tufts of grass. Now it is possible to approach the girl's remains, though from precarious footholds.

All the exposed portions of the body have been reduced to bones, but the submerged portions retain their form and substance, and bits of clothing still adhere.

Examining the remains in the mortuary at Minehead, Carter finds no fractured bones, no obvious signs of injury. And no indication of assault or stripping of clothes. The girl's coat and hat are not among the articles of clothing found.

Quickening Footsteps

Identification of the remains was swift and positive, but a harrowing experience for the girl's mother.

Whatever Mollie Phillips had been doing in crossing Codsend Moor, the place was not unknown to her. As a girl of eight she had lived for a time at Hawkington Farm cottage. But she had no friends at Hawkington at the time she disappeared.

Then had some flash of remembrance, some curiosity, drawn her back on that Sunday afternoon? A curiosity to take a walk she had known years before?

At the inquest, held at Minehead, Dr. Carter gave the cause of death as shock from exposure, with the possibility of final drowning. How did the girl get into the bog? That was the question to keep the reporters' pencils poised.

Carter proceeded to lower the temperature of anticipation. It appeared to him that the girl had pitched forward, her feet embedded in the boggy turf. He rose to give a demonstration of the manner in which he thought the girl might have fallen forward.

His next words seemed to dispose of any drama. 'There she lay; not dumped in'.

He repeated himself. 'She wasn't dumped. If anyone had

The spot on Codsend Moor, where Mollie Phillips was found.

attempted to carry that ten stone body there we should have found two bodies, not one'.

(Later, a private experiment at the spot was carried out by two heavy men, one being carried on the back of the other. There was no sinking).

Carter gave his opinion that the girl was alive when the bog received her.

Then, prompted by a juryman's question, Carter raised the temperature he had just lowered. He said the fall into the bog was more consistent with a person running. Then he modified the term to 'hurrying'.

But drama was back, and Carter, with a few colourful sentences which seemed rather in excess of his brief as a witness, said: 'The girl never intended leaving the high road. I believe she was inveigled on to this moor, that she was frightened, that she bolted in horror and tried to get off'.

Carter had created a picture at which the imaginative person could shiver.

And a mention of stones in the bog heightened the imagination. One stone, weighing 30lbs., had been pressing into the body.

But Supt. Hallett did not think it had any connection with the case. He thought that water continually running into the bog would gradually have forced the stone up against the body. If the stone had been thrown or placed on the body, it would have been under water, not on the surface.

Hallett considered the bog was dangerous. He said it was not a feasible proposition for anyone to murder the girl and then dump her body in the bog. The girl had no chance of getting out once she was in. She was only 5 feet 3 inches tall and was very plump.

The coroner, Geoffrey Clarke, told the jury they could return one of three verdicts . . . wilful murder by a person unknown, misadventure, or an open verdict.

In half an hour the jury had agreed on misadventure. But they added an opinion that Mollie Phillips had been hurrying away in fright from some person who was not necessarily near her.

Dr. Carter had been the central figure at the inquest; now the spotlight was to veer in the direction of a country parson.

And Supt. Hallett, on the brink of retirement, was almost reduced to tottering into it.

A Cry of 'Murder'

From the pulpit of Cutcombe parish church the word was 'Murder'.

Arthur Courtenay Jenoure, the stocky priest, had been at Cutcombe since 1923. He remained there obscurely until the mid-1960s, typical of the long incumbencies found in many country parishes in times past.

But Jenoure was not an obscure figure after the inquest on Mollie

Phillips, though gradually he went back to the quietude. The spotlight of publicity was swinging in his direction on Easter Saturday as he waited at his church gate to receive the coffin of Mollie Phillips. It was on him in full beam when, after reading the lesson, he mounted the pulpit.

In a voice trembling with emotion he said: 'I am quite certain that ninety per cent of the population of this district believe Mollie Phillips to have been foully murdered.

'A great many of us knew her, and we know the place where the remains were found. And yet we are asked to believe the feeble story, which might well have been culled from the pages of some nursery library, that this powerful young woman, who knew the moor well, carelessly ran into a bog, which, in all probability, at the time of the year, did not exist, and that she quietly lay there and died without a struggle.

'Insult To Intelligence'

'I am sure I am speaking in the name of the district when I say that to ask us, who knew this girl and the circumstances of her disappearance, to believe such a feeble tale as this is to offer the greatest insult to our intelligence.

'We of this neighbourhood, to put it shortly, consider the verdict of the jury would have been a disgrace to a jury of twelve year old schoolboys'.

Talking with reporters, Jenoure attacked the composition of the jury . . . . four hotel proprietors, one draper, one plumber and one garage proprietor. They were Minehead men. If one or two Exmoor people had been empanelled, said Jenoure, they would have put questions that would have absolutely floored Dr. Carter.

Jenoure expounded his theories. One was about the big stone found against the body. Jenoure argued that the stone was first placed on the girl's chest. Then, when the lower half of the body and the underclothing became saturated, it sank beneath the surface and the top part of the body was tilted up, so that the stone slid down to between the girl's legs.

According to Jenoure, the whole population of ten parishes was ready to sign a petition asking the Home Office to have the case re-opened.

The Parson Gets Support

Favourable reaction to Jenoure's pulpit outburst was widespread. Letters of support for his attitude poured in upon him.

One, 'with hearty admiration', was from authoress Beatrice Chase ('My Lady of the Moor'). She said she lived and walked alone in similar, though much wilder and more dangerous country. 'And I know that such a death is not possible. I wish people could see our Cranmere Pool country . . . that would put the fear of God into them. Yet even there we never lose a life'.

46

Beatrice said she had lived 29 years in similar country, and September was always the month when bogs and springs were lowest.

The reference to Cranmere Pool was of particular interest to Jenoure, for he had once written a dialect article mentioning the same pool. It recounted his actual experience of being able to have a picnic party in the middle of Cranmere on an August day.

Jenoure argued that if Cranmere Pool did not exist in August, the Codsend bog on Exmoor could not have trapped Mollie Phillips on a September day after a dry summer.

Codsend Wagers

In the week following the funeral police went to the Codsend bog and began to drain it preparatory to digging. They were watched by the Deputy Chief Constable (Mr. Edward Young) and Supt. Hallett.

After a dig lasting several hours the police took away something in a box. Supt. Hallett refused to say what it was.

But he did not hesitate to relate a remarkable incident that occurred while they were digging. As he said, it seemed to be a strong point in favour of the police theory.

A man on horseback, who had been following hounds, stopped about twenty yards from the scene of the dig . . . and the horse began to sink. It went into boggy ground almost up to its stomach. But, said Supt. Hallett, its rider managed to keep it on the go and it got out all right.

'It was a very funny thing that it should have happened while we were there', Hallett added.

The police were anxious to find Mollie Phillips' spectacles, a silver brooch and the buckle of her belt.

Jenoure described these as 'missing links' and said the jury should have asked questions about them at the inquest. He issued a challenge. He was prepared to allow anyone to throw him into Codsend Bog, and if he failed to get out within five minutes he would contribute £20 to a local hospital, providing his challenger would make a similar gift in the event of his being successful.

A local lad saw prospects of the bog yielding him a substantial revenue. He offered to be thrown in as often as anyone liked at a bob a time.

The police, renewing their searches on Codsend, found in the bog the girl's spectacles, belt buckle and hair slide.

The national Press were giving the case the full treatment, and Supt. Hallett complained bitterly about 'some of the rubbish' that was being printed.

But publicity was keeping the pot boiling, and the lid positively rose when it was disclosed that a Timberscombe woman had made a statement to the police. She had spoken of a man 'who had been very fond of Mollie Phillips'. The woman alleged that the man had said: 'I expect I know where Mollie Phillips is. She is not very far away'. After that the man would say nothing about the affair, and later he left the village.

The pot boiled again when a Tiverton dentist reported to the police that on the afternoon of the disappearance he saw a girl and a man struggling on the slopes of Dunkery. But the police were satisfied that the girl had not been Mollie Phillips.

Question In The House

In the House of Commons Mr. Lovat Fraser asked the Home Secretary, Mr. Clynes, if he proposed to take any action over the case. Clynes replied that if, as a result of the police inquiries, any person thought that a further inquest was desirable, application could be made to the Attorney General. And the Attorney General could make an application to the High Court, which alone had the power to order a further inquest.

The Press now stated that the girl's mother had decided to apply to the Attorney General. This was not true, but the Attorney General called for a report from the Public Prosecutor. A detective appeared in the Cutcombe district and questioned a great many people.

To the Rev. Courtenay Jenoure came a cryptic telegram mentioning the names of three people. He handed the telegram to the police.

Some tit-bit, manufactured or genuine, was now coming out every day. In the House of Commons Sir William Jowitt, the Attorney General, rose to reply to a question by Mr. Lovat Fraser.

Sir William said that on April 17th an application was made to him. It urged him to apply to the High Court for an order directing a fresh inquest into the death of Mollie Phillips.

The application was said to have been made by the mother of the dead girl.

'But I have since ascertained', said the Attorney General, 'that the applicant is a Press reporter and that he had no authority to make the application'.

Sir William then read a letter he had received from Mrs. Ford. It said she had not given her consent for an application for a fresh inquiry. 'I do not wish the case to be re-opened. I cannot stand it. I am quite satisfied with what has been done'.

The Attorney General said that Dr. Godfrey Carter, whom he called 'that eminent pathologist', had reported that all the facts were consistent with accidental death and there was no fact which pointed either to suicide or murder.

'In these circumstances', said the Attorney General, 'I do not intend to take further action in this matter'.

Job For Spilsbury

The Minehead inquest jury could draw comfort from the Attorney General's statement. Their verdict could not be upset unless fresh evidence was forthcoming.

48

There was a chance that it might. The Deputy Chief Constable announced that hair belonging to Mollie Phillips, found near the bog, had been sent to Sir Bernard Spilsbury, the famous pathologist, for examination.

In explanation to the Press, the Deputy Chief Constable referred to a statement made by a Dr. Bronte (who had been shown parts of hair) that it had been torn from a head.

'The police do not agree with this view—in fact, they believe otherwise'—said the Deputy Chief Constable. 'But in order to get an authoritative opinion to back ours we have sent the hair and two or three other articles to Sir Bernard'.

The Attorney General's statement had done nothing to damp the ardour of Cutcombe's parson. 'We shall keep the matter going', Jenoure declared. He was still getting a tremendous postbag of praise for his attitude, though he admitted that there were a few letters urging him to 'lay off'.

One letter, from a man in Wales, spoke of a 'vision' he had had. He saw 'a dark, sallow-faced man and a girl in an open shed together. They appeared to start a quarrel and the man grasped the girl around the throat. She fell to the ground and the man then took the body, dragged it up the side of a hill, and dumped it into a swamp'.

Legal Views

If any members of the Minehead jury were readers of the *Justice of the Peace and Local Government Review* they must have blushed at a letter in that journal. Written by N. W. Sibley, of Liverpool, author of *'Criminal Appeal and Evidence'*, it contended that the verdict of misadventure was not a reasonable one because of the rider the jury had added . . . that Mollie Phillips was hurrying away in fright from someone when she fell into the bog.

Verdict and rider contradicted one another, said Mr. Sibley. They were inconsistent. The jury must have thought it was a case of manslaughter, if not murder.

He quoted an observation made in 1908 by Mr. Justice Phillimore (afterwards Lord Phillimore) that 'an inconsistent verdict cannot stand'.

In a quoted case of 1909 a man had run at a woman, intending to hit her, and in consequence she jumped or fell through a window thirty feet from the ground and was killed. Mr. Justice Jelf had held that a verdict of murder might well have been returned in this case.

Was there any difference in principle, asked Sibley, between frightening a girl into a bog, where she might be drowned, and compelling someone to fall or jump from a window?

The *Justice of the Peace* had previously made its comment on the Mollie Phillips inquest. It said: 'In the total absence of evidence of what actually occurred, a fully satisfactory verdict was impossible.

But the verdict binds no-one, and in the possible event of further evidence becoming available, the person responsible can be brought to justice. For it has long been established law that if anyone, in well-founded apprehension of personal violence, does something which results in death. the person who wrongfully put him or her in fear is answerable for the consequences'.

Hallett Speaks His Mind

The end of May saw the retirement of Supt. Hallett, whose last eighteen months in the force had been the most worrisome of his career. He could not have been sorry to disappear into his new house at Minehead.

His opinion of certain sections of the national and provincial Press over their treatment of the Exmoor mystery was low. But he made it clear that he had no complaint against the local Press, whose reporting had been factual and without sensationalism. 'A great deal of the stuff that has appeared in the London papers is untrue', Hallett said. 'I and other people have been made to say a good many things that never left our lips, and that is playing a low-down game.

'For instance, when we found certain articles *IN* the bog I was made to say *AROUND* the bog, the obvious inference being that Mollie Phillips dropped them there in some sort of struggle before she got into the bog.'

Jealous of their own good relations with the police, the Taunton and West Somerset branch of the National Union of Journalists took the most unusual course of passing a resolution dissociating their members from other brethren farther afield.

Hair Not Torn

Sir Bernard Spilsbury's report on the sample of human hair now came through. It would surely apply the quietus to the Exmoor pot-boiling. Sir Bernard said: 'The almost complete absence of roots SHOWS THAT THE HAIR WAS NOT TORN FROM THE HEAD. The appearances are consistent with the hair having been bitten off by animals, such as foxes and dogs'. Spilsbury pointed out that Dr. Carter had made it clear in his report that it was impossible to determine precisely the cause of death.

Spilsbury continued: 'If she had stumbled over a boulder, her feet slipping from under her, scoring the sole of the shoe, as is quite clear, she would fall heavily into the bog, and if she was stunned she would easily be smothered as she lay face downwards. The fact that her spectacles were found near the skull indicates that she was wearing them, and supports the view that she was alive when she entered the bog.

'All the facts are consistent, in my opinion, with the view that the girl came to her death as the result of an accident, and there is no fact which points either to suicide or murder'.

Young's Last Word

The report spurred Deputy Chief Constable Young into a last statement on the case. He said: 'From the moment of the discovery of the remains we have made persistent and exhaustive inquiries into every phase and detail that would help to solve the mystery. No trouble has been too great, no stone left unturned. A detective was detailed to remain in the neighbourhood for over three weeks. An immense number of statements were taken and investigated. No evidence of foul play could be obtained, and we arrived at a conclusion which has now been confirmed by the most skilled, experienced and highly trained pathologist in the country'.

Even now Courtenay Jenoure was not silenced. 'The Mollie Phillips case is not dead', he declared. 'It is as alive as ever it was'.

In a sense Jenoure was right. The case remains alive as long as anyone who remembers it remains alive.

Those Bogs . . . Well?

The case also keeps alive the arguments over Exmoor bogs. At the end of a dry summer, was there a bog that could be a strong girl's death-trap? Some cry 'No'. They then have to consider the extraordinary incident, vouched for by a Deputy Chief Constable and a police superintendent, of a horse sinking practically to its middle, twenty yards from where the girl's remains were found.

People with a distaste for such cases as that of Mollie Phillips level the charge of sensationalism against the Press. But who coloured the picture? There was nothing about fear and flight until Carter advanced it as a theory at the inquest. And the jury endorsed the theory with their rider.

Thus was a picture created of a sinister and fatal encounter on a sunny September Sunday.

Why should Mollie Phillips be out of her way on Codsend Moor? Is it not possible that the last footsteps she took on earth were indeed the footsteps of fear?

Postscript

The title of this chapter, 'The Footsteps of Fear', represents a theory which was quite unacceptable by many Exmoor people who followed the case at the time. Some have contacted me since the first edition of this book appeared. They are at one in discounting the opinion of the experts at the inquest that Mollie Phillips was running from a pursuer and fell into the bog. They hold that she was murdered at some other spot, and that her body was carried to the bog and dumped there. An Exmoor farmer said he examined the place at the time and could see that the stones found on top of the girl's remains did not belong to the bog, but had been dislodged from a bank some distance away. Could such a clue have been missed by the police? The investigation of this case left many questions unanswered, and the Cutcombe parson's cry of 'Murder' set up echoes of endorsement which have lingered to this day.

9 Killer in a Crack

Mystery can have an oddly abstract quality. Stemming from Exmoor was the mystery of an unaccountable silence.

A silence that was to prove fatal to a man who had been enjoying a moorland holiday at a farmhouse. A silence he himself kept . . . incredibly. For a word from him, and his life might have been preserved.

It is a curious and unusual story, tracking from the moor to a cemetery; to a hospital, back again to the cemetery, and ending with a coroner's certificate that was as good as a cheque.

The fate of Alfred, a city man of 34, seems to have been decided on a moorland track on an August morning in 1935.

It was eight months later, just as a March dawn was signalling, that a mystery took shape. It settled as a black screen above Alfred's head. Its form was a tarpaulin, rigged above the grave in which this man had lain for thirty-two weeks. They were taking him up.

Exhumation creates its own peculiar shiver of mystery. There is the swearing to secrecy of the limited band who must participate at the scene . . . cemetery keepers, gravediggers, undertakers, police, perhaps a solicitor. There is the chosen time . . . between the opaque and the first pale etchings in the dawn sky, when the tombstones struggle for recognition.

It was four a.m. on March 14th, 1936, when they started to raise Alfred. They drove him to the hospital at Minehead, where he had died on August 14th of the previous year.

Pathologists Sir Bernard Spilsbury and Dr. Godfrey Carter were waiting for him.

Speechless

Alfred had come to Exmoor at the beginning of August, 1935, and was staying at a farmhouse. He was having a typical moorland holiday . . . riding, walking, good eating, a bit of lazing.

But on August 6th he awoke feeling unwell. He had toothache. He found difficulty in swallowing, and he could not eat his breakfast. His symptoms persisted, and the next day he went over to Brendon to consult a doctor. Alfred complained about his 'swallow'. He was unable fully to open his mouth, so a thorough examination of the back of his throat was impossible. He mentioned that he was subject to attacks of quinsy, and his condition was put down to this. The next day he was still in discomfort and the doctor came over from Brendon to see him.

Alfred had a slight temperature. The difficulty with opening the mouth was still apparent, but an examination of the jaw disclosed no malformation. However, it was decided to send Alfred to hospital.

At Minehead Hospital the surgeon received the patient as a case of acute tonsilitis. By this time he was unable to speak, and the surgeon took a history of the case by means of question and answer on paper. No examination of the throat could be made because the man was now unable to open his mouth at all. There was swelling on both sides of the neck and under the chin, and breathing was being achieved only with difficulty. Next day Alfred managed to open his mouth sufficiently for a swab to be taken. It was negative.

The third day. Swelling of neck and chin had spread to the chest. Alfred was now diagnosed as a case of acute sepsis, not, however, of diphtheric origin. The latter had been indicated by the negative swab. The treatment given included a new drug, brontosil.

But this man was dying. His general condition was weakening. Now his heart was affected. Death came on August 14th. The certificate issued showed it to be primarily due to Ludwig's angina, with acute tonsilitis as a leading-up cause.

Alfred was buried in Minehead cemetery. There he lay until they raised him in the chill dawn of a March day, eight months later. Why?

Found Something

Exhumation is sufficiently rare for it to claim the headlines when it occurs. The drama of official disinterment, with its privacy and stealth, is never divorced in the public mind from the age-old revulsion against interfering with the dead. It is a resort requiring Home Office sanction and usually foreshadows trouble; often a crime investigation.

But this case was going to be different. Why exhumation? Because somebody had spoken . . . rather late. Somebody who, at a coroner's inquiry into how Alfred came by his death, said he had spoken before.

But nobody seemed to have heard him then. And Alfred himself had not spoken at all, even when he was still capable of opening his mouth.

The day was still young when in the mortuary of Minehead Hospital Dr. Godfrey Carter, watched by Sir Bernard Spilsbury, set to work. Carter quickly found something, and Spilsbury nodded wisely.

There was no need to detain Alfred any longer. He was returned to the grave from which he had been taken but a few hours before.

Doctors In The Dark

Alfred had really begun his strange dying on a moorland track on the morning of August 5, 1935.

His case can be written as the mystery of 'Nothing Was Said'.

Alfred, out riding, had fallen from his horse. Eight months later, at the post mortem examination, Godfrey Carter was to find a fracture of the lower jaw. Through the crack in the bone a killing germ had entered.

Now Alfred had been riding with another man, who was also a guest at the farmhouse. He had gone to Alfred's aid after the latter's fall. He gave evidence at the inquest following the exhumation that he had spoken about Alfred's fall at the time.

But no-one at the farmhouse could remember that he had.

And the almost incredible feature was that Alfred himself, suffering so much discomfort in jaw and neck, never mentioned the fall to the doctors who examined him. They were left to diagnose in the dark.

Yet the fall must have been mentioned by someone, after a lapse of time. Alfred's father heard about it; his solicitors contacted the coroner, asked for an exhumation, and the Home Office granted it.

But the real reason for exhumation would not be made public until the coroner's inquiry. Exhumation orders are not granted unless special reasons can be shown. In this case the reasons were not sinister, but they were of unusual interest. They had been explained to the coroner.

Why It Mattered

Alfred was dead, plainly not through foul play, so what purpose could exhumation serve? Did it matter whether he had died from the cause that was written on the death certificate, or from a condition brought about by a fractured jaw sustained in a fall?

It mattered very much. For when Dr. Carter pronounced at the inquest that death was due to acute cellulitis of the neck, consequent upon a fracture of the jaw, it meant an inquest verdict of Accidental Death.

Accident or natural causes . . . again, did it matter? Yes, because an insurance company, with whom Alfred had had a policy, would have to pay out £1,000 if he came by his death as the result of an accident. And now it was shown that he had.

The insurance company had disputed their liability when a claim was made upon them. Small wonder. An accident? About which nothing had been heard? About which not even the victim had spoken? There was certainly no reference to an accident on the original death certificate, and in the insurance business only a death certificate has the words that count.

Now, the insurance men could be satisfied. In the words of the coroner it was 'a very curious case'. It was certainly a strange mystery of silence . . . particularly the victim's.

A word in time . . . and there would have been no need to disturb a man in his grave.

The clods were shovelled for a second time upon the coffin of the man who had come to Exmoor for his last holiday. The case of the £1,000 exhumation was closed.

10 The Bones of Kinsford

A startled Albert Wyatt reined his pony and looked down from the saddle.

At three heaps of charred bones.

And he had an uneasy feeling that he was looking at human remains. Why three little heaps? It looked to Wyatt as if someone had thrown the bones from a receptacle, a small quantity at a time.

Wyatt dismounted for a closer look. Now he could distinguish fragments of a backbone, a rib and a skull. And there were pieces of metal that looked like steel splinters.

Someone was coming along the road. Wyatt turned to see John Thorne, of Bentwitchen. 'Here', he said, 'look at this'.

Thorne looked . . . and supported Wyatt's opinion. These were surely human remains.

Exmoor was about to project the mystery of the Kinsford Cross bones.

Strangers Allotment

It was Sunday, May 10th, 1936, when Wyatt rode from his home at Higher Fyldon Farm, North Molton, to Kinsford Cross, where he made his disquieting discovery. The location was Strangers Allotment, a rough and boggy enclosure running parallel with the Simonsbath—Yarde Down road, and sloping from the border line down to Kinsford Water. It was just within the Somerset border of Exmoor.

55

The spot was lonely, the nearest habitation being at Kinsford Water, nearly a mile away. Here lived Bob Ellis, a former huntsman of the Exmoor Foxhounds. From the front of his house the whole of Strangers Allotment was in view.

Thirty paces from a gate giving entrance to the allotment from the Simonsbath road . . . and there were the heaps of bones. In them, was there the shape of a murky mystery?

It was a place Farmer Wyatt rarely visited, except when he was summering sheep there. He rode over from Higher Fyldon Farm, two miles away, on May 8th, to check that the fences were in good order; prior to that day he had not been to Strangers for six months. On May 8th one of his men, Jim Squire, was with him. Neither man saw any bones then. They were at Strangers again the following day, mending fences. Again, no bones.

But the following day, there they lay.

Wyatt went immediately to the police. The area was combed, and the police interviewed many people, including Bob Ellis, but he could not help. He had seen nothing unusual taking place on Strangers.

The bones were giving pathologist Godfrey Carter a headache. That is, if human remains are ever really capable of worrying people who live by examining them. Carter was immediately certain that the bones were human, but he wanted another opinion on certain peculiarities, so he contacted the renowned anatomist, Professor J. E. S. Frazer, of St. Mary's Hospital, London.

Master's Experiment

At Huish's Grammar School, Taunton, science master Cyril Rutt, known to generations of boys as Ginger, was busy with a chemistry lesson. Ginger hailed from West Somerset, his mother having been headmistress of the tiny wayside school of Elworthy, on the Watchet-Wiveliscombe road.

Ginger had a visitor, who spoke on a very private matter. As a result, Ginger disappeared into the school lab to make an experiment. He was expected to come up with an answer . . . for the police.

Detective Inspector Eric Webber, of Somerset Constabulary H.Q., was ferreting, but not in the hedge-banks of Exmoor. He had a shrewd idea about the Kinsford mystery, but the next move depended on what Ginger Rutt might have to tell him.

The answer came. It was what Webber had hoped for. Now, with Rutt's information and the reports of Dr. Carter and Professor Frazer, Webber believed he could prise open the mystery. But days of patient and quiet inquiries lay ahead.

One other person had to be in on this . . . the coroner.

Meanwhile, the Press were besieging the police for information, and the West Somerset coroner, Geoffrey Clarke, was also being bothered, so much so that on May 27th he made an announcement.

The Moorland at Kinsford.

He did it while conducting an inquest (nothing to do with the Exmoor affair) at Wellington. Clarke said the Kinsford bones were human. He then remarked upon the many inquiries he had been getting from Pressmen, and added: 'If it is necessary to hold an inquest on these remains the Press will be given 24 hours notice'.

The Missing Middle

On July 24th the coroner drove to Simonsbath to hold an inquest on the remains. On the information now available to him he need not have held an inquiry, but he intended to allay public anxiety.

It was an inquest conclusive in verdict but with a chunk of information missing. It gave the public a beginning and an end, but no middle.

And curiosity must for ever remain unsatisfied, for part of the evidence was taken in camera.

The coroner sat in Simonsbath Post Office, with a jury composed of six Exmoor farmers and the village postmaster. In those days it was the custom to hold inquests as close as convenient to the scene of a tragedy, and in this respect every district coroner was a much travelled man. He might 'sit upon' a body in a cottage where the death had occurred, and might have walked there across a couple of fields. Or he might face his jury across a farmhouse table.

Detective Inspector Webber slipped into the room carrying a small suitcase. He opened it to display the Kinsford bones.

They resembled, said Godfrey Carter, fragments of every portion of the human skeleton.

A report on the bones had been drawn up by Professor Frazer. It was astounding in its detail, said the coroner, and so technical that there was no point in reading it to the jury.

They were shown the bones, and that alone, said the coroner, should make them realise what Dr. Carter and Professor Frazer had been up against in the early stages of these inquiries.

'*There have been suggestions that this was a very carefully planned murder*', said the coroner . . . and promptly called Detective Inspector Webber to show that it wasn't.

No Criminal Offence

Webber proceeded to pick the mystery to pieces, up to a point where he withheld his hand on the coroner's instructions. The inquiry then continued in camera. One piece of the mystery would remain veiled.

Webber wiped out murder when he said that the condition and disposition of the bones appeared to indicate that there had not been an attempt to dispose of a body following the commission of a criminal offence.

But mystery was sustained as Webber spoke of a quantity of thick metal scale being intimately mixed with the bones, and splashes of fusible metal upon some pieces of bone.

This was where science master Rutt had come into the case. He had been asked by the police to analyse pieces of the metal scale found with the bones. He had pronounced it to be scale from iron which had been subjected to long, intense heat.

And that heat had been created by a fierce draught of air. Rutt decided that the fuel used to produce such heat was neither coal nor wood, but probably coal gas.

Ah! It was now obvious what kind of place Webber would have looked for after receiving Rutt's report. The mystery itself was on the way to disintegration.

Of course. Webber had carried his investigations to a crematorium.

The Kinsford bones were the remains of a lawfully cremated person. Police and coroner now knew who it was. And the identity of the person who had deposited the bones on Strangers Allotment was also known.

In the presence of Detective Inspector Webber the coroner had given an undertaking to the family concerned that identities would be kept secret.

It was, the coroner told the jury, reasonable to give such an undertaking.

So a portion of the inquest had to be conducted in private. But for the open record, Webber was allowed to say: 'I know the circumstances in which the bones were deposited, and I know who put them there'.

Never Again

Whatever the personal reasons behind the placing of the bones on Exmoor, it was to be hoped that it would never happen again, and with this in mind the coroner asked Webber: 'Is there any likelihood that remains cremated nowadays could be disposed in conditions similar to this'?

Several speculations arise from such a question. But police officers and coroner did not have to speculate. They knew the full facts.

Webber's answer to the coroner was that there was no chance of a repitition of the incident. 'I understand that precautions have been taken against that', he added.

Was it a case of someone being able to claim a relative's bones from a crematorium before the whole process of cremation had been completed? For the reasons explained, the story has a gap.

The police may have been half on to the answer to the Kinsford mystery from the start. As Detective Inspector Webber said: 'To reduce the human body to the condition in which this one was found is extremely difficult. No reasonable person who had committed an offence and wanted to dispose of the body would, if he had been successful in getting it to that condition, have finished up by depositing the remains in an open field on the surface of the ground, when about five minutes more work would have reduced the remains to powder'.

11 Phantoms Afoot: Spectres Awheel

Thump of drum and pounding of piano keys. The heat of a
'hop' at Wheddon Cross on a night in 1929.

Two girls, one a nurse, slip out into the darkness some time
before the dance is due to end. They have to return to their village
of Timberscombe and they do not want to be too late home. Before
them stretches the long, winding down-fall of Cutcombe Hill.

The brash and the brave may give Cutcombe Hill and its creeps
the scornful brush-off, but now and again in the still of night the
old gradient replies by flicking the feather of fear along the spine
of the nervy.

And then the Rest-and-be-Thankful at the top of the hill can be
the Reach-and-be-Thankful!

Let the night grow late. Let the walker exchange the company
of Wheddon Cross, perhaps the **Rest-and-be-Thankful,** or the dance
hall for the lonely, tree-sighing **highway** that belonged once to
the coach and four.

Then the twin eyes of an upward sweeping car are an approaching
comfort. But they pass, and the loneliness presses in again.

And suppose the next vehicle is unlighted, a shapeless, advancing
dread!

Our girl walkers turn about. They pound back up the slope,
not daring to look round. They burst into the dance hall and pant
their story. Listeners, older folk, nod with the wisdom of recollection of stories handed down. Could the two frightened girls have
seen that **something** on Cutcombe Hill?

Reader's Choice

A chapter on the ghosts and phantoms of Exmoor or, for that
matter, of anywhere, belongs naturally to the category of mystery.
It can be read with amusement, scepticism or frank disbelief, but
its entertainment value is enhanced if the reader is prepared to
co-operate in the manner suggested by a well-known authoress, who
counselled 'the willing suspension of disbelief'.

Once that essential state of rapport has been achieved, which
means that the reader has bent a little, though not entirely back-
wards, there should be no difficulty in travelling weightlessly over
Exmoor with all manner of ghosts and phantoms in tow; the
charming and the chilling, even the beautiful. Gliding ladies,
bobbing little men, bellringing monks; as many, in fact, as might
be conveniently carried in the phantom hearse of Cutcombe Hill
or the phantom coach between Luckwell Bridge and Stone Cross
(last reported sighting 1953!).

An Exmoor mist is a grey phantom of itself; roll it back, and an old shepherd in a long cloak may be standing at Comer's Gate; a tall beech hedge waves up and down to bring terror to a horse.

Death-Coach

Because those girls turned tail and ran back to Cutcombe on that night in 1929 they may have denied themselves a full sight of the phantom hearse of Cutcombe Hill. The death-coach story is retailed, with variations, in a good many places. It is not sufficiently ubiquitous to be a national heritage in the phantom line, but Cutcombe Hill claims the coach, Marque I, in all its trappings . . . the soundless wheels and horses' hooves, the accompanying black hound, the nodding plumes. What is the coach doing on the road, but gathering up its load of souls of the newly dead?

The incident with the girls from the dance was recorded in several newspapers, but the most publicised story of the phantom hearse of Cutcombe Hill was in the last quarter of the 19th century. It followed the hair-raising experience of a Winsford farmer who boasted, during a wining and dining session at a hostelry one night that he would later drive his gig down Cutcombe Hill and into Minehead.

Very late, the ostler of the Luttrell Arms at Dunster was astonished to see galloping up the street towards him a horse with a gig, but no driver. The horse was soaked with sweat; its eyes filled with terror. A search party went out along the Cutcombe road. There on the hill they found the farmer flat on his face. Not a word could they get out of him then, and never would he speak thereafter of what he had seen.

Local people said it must have been the phantom hearse. The incident awoke the muse of a person who treated it with some levity in fourteen, four-line verses, two of which declared that the farmer never again ventured out after dark unless accompanied by his wife. For:

Well he knew if phantom hearse
Should chance to come their way,
His wife would scare the bogey worse
Than it could her dismay!

The wife must have possessed a face like the back of the traditional bus . . . or, in this case, hearse.

If everybody said, as did a grinning Exmoor character: 'Phantoms? Gid out wi' ee. I never zeed nuthin wuss than meself', ghosts and phantoms would never get off the ground and into the records.

Four-In-Hand

Mercifully for writers, there are people who, if they have seen things 'worse than themselves', are prepared to say so. One man, known to the author, had no hesitation in telling a colleague journalist of an unnerving experience on the Cutcombe—Exford road on a

December day in 1953, and he did not mind his impressions going into print. He said he saw the phantom coach and four between Luckwell Bridge and Stone Cross. The place is known as Langdon's Way, where a sharp bend received straightening treatment many years ago. For traffic going towards Exford the road dips towards the bend and then there is an upward slope.

The man is, by reason of his professional work, well known over a considerable area. Here are his own words: 'At ten in the morning I was driving my car towards Exford. There was quite a thick fog. Just as I was going down the slope towards the bend, at not more than ten miles an hour, I saw something coming right at me down the other slope, and I recognised it as a stage coach with four horses. The impression was extremely vivid. There was no sound, but I could see the breath coming from the horses' nostrils as they snorted, and the driver sitting stolidly on his box. It was so close that the thought went through my mind, 'Good Lord, I've had it', and I pulled up with a jerk. But the coach and horses came right on and through my car. I looked behind me and there was absolutely nothing to be seen'.

The point where the coach and four appeared was where the old road used to run. Might it have been Squire Musgrave's coach? Musgrave was a flamboyant character of the 18th century. He lived at Stone Lodge, and tradition says he drives his coach and four on the Exford—Cutcombe road.

One inference to be drawn is that Exmoor's vehicular phantoms do not observe the Highway Code or the regulations for lighting-up time.

Pedestrian Ghosts

These have always outnumbered the vehicular, for the simple reason that they cannot all get into the phantom coaches. And they may not approve of group hauntings. This is all to the good in the case of the lovely lady who walks at Red Post, Porlock, for her pedestrian habits have allowed her grace of bearing, beauty of appearance and apparel, to be seen in the clearest detail.

Amos Brown, a fine craftsman in stone (take a look at Malmsmead Bridge) was always regarded as a most reliable reporter of the Lovely Lady in the Spotted Dress down in the vale.

The name Red Post may relate to the ruins of a very old house, or its entrance gate, built of red sandstone near the branch road to Luccombe. Late one night Amos Brown, who had been working overtime on a farm, was returning to Porlock. It was bright moonlight, so bright that, in Brown's words, 'you could see to pick up a pin'. As he approached Red Post he saw a lady coming towards him. Every detail of her appearance was clearly visible. She wore a gleaming white silk gown, darkly spotted; her head was bare, and her hair fell over her shoulders. Brown was rooted to the spot; he felt no fear, he said, only wonderment that a lovely lady should

62

be out alone so late. The figure turned towards the shadows where the old house had stood . . . and vanished.

Brown was not the only viewer of loveliness in the light of the moon. Some time after, one William Holsworthy saw the figure and made bold to bid her 'Good evening' and ask, out of regard for her safety, if he should accompany her to wherever she was going. The lady made no response, and in a few moments she had merged with the deep shadows. Her appearances were frequent, and children in the Brown family were in the habit of asking their elders, 'Have you seen the lovely lady in the spotted dress to-night'?

Shivery

The most shivery story is one mentioned by the Rev. W. H. Thornton in his *Reminiscences of an Old West Country Clergyman.* One morning he heard that Mrs. Mary Stenner, of Selworthy, had seen a ghost the night before. Thornton went to see her and found her not far from a state of collapse. She told him:

'I hadn't left Budleigh Hill by two gunshots when there it was, the nasty thing, running along by my side. 'Twas awful. It had four legs and it was black, and had great fiery eyes as big as saucers, and it ran on until it came to where the water crosses under the road, and they things, o'course, never can abide running water, so it just couldn't get across, and off it went up into the air like a flash of fire. I screeched—oh! I screeched'.

Thornton saw John Hobbs, the sexton, who took the story most calmly. 'I know all about it', he said. "Tis exactly twenty-five years since we was bringing a corpse from Horner Mill to Selworthy, and the handle of the coffin against the head came loose, just exactly to the very spot where Mary Stenner met with the ghost last night. I picked up a stone and knocked the handle in again, and no doubt it went into the corpse's brain and let the spirit out. Oh yes! I know all about it'.

Sydenham's Return

The celebrated Samuel Johnson made a comment of typical pith on the subject of ghosts: it was that the world had been going a long time, but 'still it is undecided whether or not there has ever been an instance of the spirit of any person appearing after death. All argument is against it; but all belief is for it'.

It would be interesting to know whether or not Johnson, who was born in 1708, twenty years after the 'event', ever heard or read of the most classic ghost story of Exmoor, the return of Major George Sydenham, of Combe, Dulverton, three weeks after his death.

Johnson could have read about it, for an account of the Sydenham manifestation was given in a treatise on the soul of man, published towards the end of the 17th century and written by a Doctor of Divinity, the Rev. John Flavel.

Few stories of the supernatural have been so respected or so well-attested. Through the centuries the Sydenham families and their seats—Combe at Dulverton, Brimpton near Yeovil and Combe Sydenham, Monksilver—have contributed a great deal of interest to romance and local history.

Major George Sydenham, who was living at Combe, Dulverton, in the 1680s, had a great friend, Capt. Dyke, then living at Pixton. Both men had been prominent soldiers for Charles I during the Civil War. In their conversations they argued much about the Being of God and the immortality of the soul. Sydenham took the line that there was no future existence; Dyke held the opposite view. They agreed that whoever died first should appear to the other . . . if permitted.

Sydenham was the first to go, in 1688 at Banbury. Three weeks later he appeared to Dyke in the latter's bedroom. Dyke emerged in the morning 'in a visage and form much differing from himself; with his eyes staring and his whole body shaking and trembling' (words from the Rev. John Flavel's treatise).

Dyke said to a friend: 'I have seen the major. If ever I saw him in my life I saw him but now, this morning after it was light. He came to my bedside and he said, 'I am come to tell you that there is a God and a very just and terrible one, and if you do not turn over a new leaf you will find it so''.

Respect

The respect in which successive generations of the Sydenham family held this story seems evident from a letter Dr. George F. Sydenham, of happy Dulverton memory, wrote to the *West Somerset Free Press* in December, 1921. There had been some rather sceptical writing about the Sydenham ghost in a feature article in this newspaper, and Dr. Sydenham took exception to what he called 'fun being poked at my ancestor's appearance after death'.

The doctor, in his day one of the most colourful characters of Dulverton and the moorland, wrote: 'It is not a matter of public interest to relate what I have seen and what has been related to me by others worthy of credence. But the appearance of Major George Sydenham is a matter of history and therefore is of public interest'.

The liberality of tradition supplies numerous Exmoor ghosts. For instance, the headless sow running with a litter near Wellshead, Exford. One may be told of the shivery indefinable, usually called *a something*! There is *a something* that came up a lane from Hill, near Downscombe, and caused the death of a man who had agreed to be tied to a tree so that he would just have to stop and see what the *something* was! There is *a something*, an uneasy sensation at some of the old barrow mounds.

To all unnamed, unclassified spectres who may feel peeved at their omission from this chapter, the author makes tremulous apology.

12 'Watch The Wall, My Darling'

. . . 'while the gentlemen go by'.

Peter Bond was a man who saw more than was good for him.

Perhaps, after he had been publicly flogged through the streets of Minehead (100 lashes) he decided to see less of what was going on privately.

Exmoor dips ponderous and rocky toes into the sea. Up to the mid 19th century the intersection of combes running down from the heights to secluded bays were of a different class of 'amenity value' than they are to-day. They meant a certain kind of business, of which, if people knew, they did not speak. It was best to treat that business as the mystery of the night . . . the muffled oars, the trotting ponies, the creaking carts.

Smuggling! Really no mystery; rather the thrill of stealth. For everyone knew smuggling was going on, and the receivers of the gains from 'free trade' were representative of the whole strata of society, from the rich man in his castle to the poor man at his cottage gate.

Liquor had a better taste when untainted with excise duty, and after a smack of the lips over a nightcap the bed was more comfortable to the body between sheets of Irish linen that had come ashore without the knowledge of the King's officers.

It was easy for the night-runners to conceal their contraband in the wild country of Exmoor, and smuggling was taking place on a prodigious scale from the time of Charles II until well into the 19th century. The beginning of a gradual diminution was seen when Pitt the Younger reduced the high duty on goods from overseas. Better a guaranteed return for the Revenue than the extent of the free trade. For Pitt calculated in 1784 that of 13 million pounds of tea consumed in this country, only $5\frac{1}{2}$ millions had paid duty.

Aroma

There is plenty of evidence of duty-free tea coming ashore in the Exmoor area, but the keen aroma of smuggling seems to depend more on brandy and tobacco! Smuggling was just a venal sin; no more was thought of it by operators and receivers than is thought to-day of a mild fiddle with the income-tax form.

The smuggling game was stretched along the Somerset and North Devon coast, from Ilfracombe in the west to Weston-super-Mare in the east. It was played in the combes and caves of the Exmoor seaboard, which so lends itself to the traditional picture of contraband landings; it was played, with the operational variations of necessity, upon the open beaches of the flatter shores to the east; and with defiant daring in the ports of Minehead and Watchet.

It is a picture which ranges from an old man with a donkey, waiting on a path at Glenthorne in the west for the signals of an approaching schooner; past the 'phantom hearse' of Blue Anchor (a smugglers' cooked story to keep people from prying), to the Breton captain who failed to realise that the tide went out too far at Weston, so that he stranded his lugger, leaving the shore dotted with the buoyed kegs that had been dropped overboard to await collection.

The Night-Walker

Peter Bond was a Minehead shoemaker. His story is a three-fold illustration of smuggling; its extent; connivance in it by gentry and business people; and the measures taken, under a masquerade of justice, to shut the mouths of informers.

In 1682 Charles II sent his Surveyor-General of Customs, William Culliforde, to West Somerset to investigate what was euphemistically called free trading, with particular reference to the ports of Minehead and Watchet. Culliforde was horrified by his findings, not least at the connivance of local revenue officers with the smugglers.

Peter Bond, of whom a public example was to be made later, by whipping him through the streets, swore information to Culliforde. Although this was 1682, Bond went under a label that had been, in many cases unjustly, attached to his kind since the 15th century— that of 'common night-walker, eavesdropper, spy (on neighbours) and disturber of the peace'. In its narrowed context it meant that Bond was often about when wiser citizens were abed, and he was likely to see more than was good for him or for the comfort of those engaged in free trade.

Minehead had two port officials or 'tydsmen', James Hellier and Henry Clement. Hellier was the principal. Culliforde rumbled him as 'a very cunning fellow who hath governed the port many years to His Majesty's prejudice'.

Churchwarden In It

Night-walker Peter Bond had made startling disclosures, and not only about James Hellier. He had named a prominent Minehead merchant, Thomas Wilson, who was also a churchwarden.

According to the information Bond gave, tydsman Hellier was on duty one night when a Bristol vessel put into port. And Hellier did nothing to prevent 40 packets of cloth being carried from the ship to the back wall of Thomas Wilson's house on the quay. Bond also told Culliforde that he had seen wine and brandy landed and taken to the cellars of Samuel Crockford and Isaac Davis, and Irish linen to the quayside stable of Robert Seager. All the time, said Bond, those rascals Hellier and Clement were walking the street to see that the coast was clear.

Bond might have laid some of his information with impunity

Smugglers' Cottage in Porlock.

against smaller fry. But in dragging in the name of Thomas Wilson he had gone too far. He must be stopped at all costs.

So a brother merchant of Thomas Wilson, named Richard Start, went to Col. Luttrell, the chief magistrate, and applied for a warrant against Bond, on the complaint that Bond was 'a night-walker for whose activities it is impossible *for honest merchants to do their business'!* Such rogues as Bond, Start said, should be publicly whipped for a warning to other rogues.

Bond was kept in jail for five days, and the magistrates ordered him to be publicly whipped through the streets. No-one among Minehead folk could be found to wield the lash, and Col. Luttrell had to send one of his own staff . . . it was probably the coachman . . . to administer the whipping.

Dairy Hole

Porlock Weir smuggling robbed the customs of a lot of revenue. Many temporary hiding places for illicit goods have been discovered in the area since smuggling died out. At Higher Doverhay Farm there was a 'hide' between an inner and an outer wall. A second wall had been built outside the main wall of the house at the dairy end. The thatched roof was brought down to cover the space between the two. The new wall therefore looked from the outside like the main wall of the house. The 'hide' was approached from the dairy through a small opening which could be concealed by placing a milk pan before it.

It was near Porlock that another hiding place was exposed during a foxhounds run, a hound having disappeared down a hole in the middle of a field.

Ghostly Cortege

Running contraband under the eyes of conniving revenue officers in a port seems to lack the traditional atmosphere of smuggling . . . best expressed in the lonely beach, the muffled oars, the crunch of a footstep on shingle, and the waiting waggons.

So let us to the flat shore east of Minehead . . . at Blue Anchor . . . though not to look, for that would mean death within a year. This was the story the smugglers put out to dissuade anyone with inquisitive tendencies. On any dark night, it was said, between midnight and the small hours of the morning, a ghostly cortege consisting of two horses, a hearse with nodding plumes and coffin might leave the beach and proceed inland. Look, and you die ere twelve months have passed. With superstition so rife in the first half of the 19th century, no-one was going to risk a premature end by looking upon a phantom hearse. The 'cortege', of course, was of familiar substance . . . two horses and a farm waggon loaded with packages. There is a story of the waggon losing a wheel as it went through a village. The men in charge quietly knocked up the local blacksmith, who did a quick repair job and was handed a cask of brandy . . . a guarantee of his contentment and silence.

Caves

The atmosphere of smuggling hangs above the wave rolling to the mouth of a cave. The caves along the rocky coast from Minehead, past Hurtstone Point and the Exmoor cliffs are naturals as smuggling links, and a few may have been enlarged by human hand in the smuggling days. One is under Hurtstone Point. It is accessible only at low water. It runs back several hundred yards, and a coastguard who went in as far as he dared expressed the opinion that the cave did not owe its size entirely to the action of the natural forces. An old Selworthy story has it that a passage from Selworthy church leads into this cave, but it must be submitted that not even the most Herculean of smugglers would have undertaken such a task of excavation.

Just west of Minehead, and below Burgundy combe, there was a cave marked on an old map as Smugglers' Doom. It fell in about sixty years ago.

Wishfully, almost, one always associates caves with smuggling. Conan Doyle helped us there. In his novel, 'Micah Clarke', the hero is captured by a gang of smugglers in the Quantock district and taken to their hiding place, a large cave in a wild gorge in the hills. From a concealed entrance a long, winding passage, cut through solid rock, opened into a lofty and roomy cave, the roof of which was hung with long lime crystals sparkling and gleaming in the light of a huge fire and wall torches. The cave was described as leading down to the seashore, because Micah could hear the booming and splashing of the waves.

Unfortunately for the wishful thinkers and would-be discoverers, Conan Doyle was using his imagination entirely in giving this description.

Skeleton

One of the westernmost links with smuggling along the Exmoor coast is Chambercombe Farm, near Ilfracombe. Once the manor house of Chambercombe, it keeps a grim story. In 1865, when some repairs were being made to the house, the outline of what had been a window was discovered, yet it did not appear to relate to a room. Investigation was made, and a room was discovered between two others. On the remains of a bedstead lay the skeleton of a woman. It is supposed that she was a Spanish lady who survived a wreck near Hele, only to be captured by smugglers and conveyed through a secret passage existing between Chambercombe Farm and Hele beach. The story says that she was robbed and left to die of starvation.

In Smugglers' Days.

Brandy Path

Far below the high road meeting place of Somerset and Devon, at County Gate, the Rev. W. S. Halliday, in 1830, built the lovely house of Glenthorne, a few yards above the waves and reached by three miles of zig-zag track falling from the A.39 road. At the same time Mr. Halliday converted to a road a path on those steep slopes. It had been given, and with good reason, the name of Brandy Path. Here, an old man, a link between incoming contraband and reception, would lie, night after night, his only companion a donkey, on whose back was rigged a triangle of three lanthorns showing out to sea. Eventually the signal would be matched by the three triangled lights of the contraband schooner coming into Glenthorne to land her cargo. The old man used to complain that his night on the path chilled him to the marrow, but it must be presumed that the appropriate de-freezing medicine was sometimes available.

Lugger Ahoy

The times lent themselves to smooth smuggling. The wagon of the 1800s, coming from the beach at Blue Anchor, would not be meeting a police Panda car, and the schooner standing off at sea was in no danger of interception by a fast motor launch. Sailing from the Bristol Channel ports to anywhere between Brest and Hamburg, also to Spain and Portugal, was a large fleet, mainly schooners, in which Minehead and Watchet owners were well represented. If the skippers and crews were unable to find all their requirements in the ports they visited, opportunities frequently presented themselves on the homeward voyage. Dodging about to the south'ard of Land's End, well outside the three-mile limit, or may be in the broad mouth of the Bristol Channel, were the famous luggers, whose superb sailing qualities in the hands of the skilful seamen of the Breton and Normandy coasts were the envy of many skippers of tubs engaged in the home trade. A hail from a schooner and a courteous inquiry for 'Le Capitaine' often led to mutual recognition. The homeward bound schooner hove to, and there was a quick transfer of 'provisions' from the lugger.

By reason of their speed and the daring of their crews, the luggers would often venture well up channel, and this enabled the small coasting craft of the Somerset shore to bring home contraband.

One lugger captain overplayed his hand when he came up as far as Weston-super-Mare. He ran well into the bay and pitched overboard and buoyed his cargo. He did not know how far the tide went out. To his horror, as dawn broke, the lugger was lying high and dry on the mud, with her cargo strewn around her. Never was there a more welcome sight for the local excisemen.

The last of Kipling's mysterious 'gentlemen' has gone by and around the corner of time. 'Brandy for the parson, baccy for the clerk'. And pickings for people who pretended smuggling was a mystery.

13 The Dog it was that died

The town of Minehead is called the 'Gateway to Exmoor National Park'. In that gateway, on the morning of November 20th, 1978 representatives of the television and newspaper world took station in force. The public, too, were swarming.

Never had a country magistrates' court been so besieged by Press and public as was Minehead's that morning. The proceedings just starting would entail sensational and bizarre evidence and end in the committal of four men for trial at the Old Bailey . . . a trial to which the chief prosecutor would apply the analogy of 'A Greek or Shakespearean tragedy'. In the public anticipation it would be the 'trial of the century'. It had all begun a long while before as an Exmoor mystery.

. . . . . .

It was around nine o'clock on the night of October 24th, 1975 when Ted Lethaby, an AA patrolman of Countisbury, was driving his car on the coast road towards Porlock. By the turning to Yenworthy Lodge Farm a man stood in the road, waving his arms. Ted Lethaby stopped. Lying against the bank was the still warm body of a big black dog, a Great Dane. It had been shot through the head. It was the pet of the man in the road, Norman Scott, aged 35, who was then living at Combe Martin. Frightened and hysterical, Scott babbled to the patrolman that an attempt had just been made to kill him because he knew something about Jeremy Thorpe and was going to put it into a book.

The Rt. Hon. Jeremy Thorpe, Privy Councillor, Liberal Party leader, was M.P. for North Devon.

To Ted Lethaby the incident sounded 'like James Bond stuff . . . not the kind of thing you expect on Exmoor'. Those were his words to a *West Somerset Free Press* reporter who interviewed him. The pistol shot that killed Scott's dog, Rinka, was to echo sensationally in corridors of power and throughout the land, even overseas. From that Exmoor road a 'James Bond' kind of story would creep tortuously along the byways of communication to a final dénouement in Number One Court at the Old Bailey . . . a story alleging conspiracy and incitement to murder.

For the moment, all was mystery . . . as thick as an Exmoor fog. The *West Somerset Free Press*, of which I was then Editor, published as much about the affair as could be gleaned from normal enquiries. The police appeared to be unusually cagey over the release of information.

The people of Porlock were wondering. On the night of the incident their village was sealed off while police checked on motorists. They were looking for a man who had been in a Ford Escort car with Norman Scott and his dog, but he was now clear of the area.

With this man, later identified as Andrew Gino Newton, an airline pilot, Scott had been driven to Porlock, and they had talked in the Castle Hotel. On the return journey they stopped near Yenworthy Lodge Farm entrance. They got out. Then, said Scott, Newton shot the dog through the head with a pistol, which he then pointed at Scott, saying, 'Now it's your turn'. The pistol appeared to jam. Newton cursed it and got back into the car and drove off, leaving Scott weeping over the body of his dog.

Why, it may be asked, was Scott riding in a car with someone whom, he alleged, had tried to shoot him? It would emerge that Newton originally turned up in North Devon and had gained Scott's confidence by pretending to be his protector against people who were trying to kill him.

In 1974 Scott had come to live in the Barnstaple district and had filled public house ears with a story alleging that he and Jeremy Thorpe had a homosexual relationship in the 1960s.

. . . . . .

Soon after the Exmoor incident I was visited in my office by a prominent Liberal of the Bridgwater constituency. I formed the impression that this was a 'feeler' call. Sure enough, my visitor steered his way to 'this funny business on Exmoor'. Would my paper be following it up? he asked. Only if it had a court sequel, was my answer. We would not be investigating a background of rumour.

Subsequently, I was surprised to receive a telephone call from Jeremy Thorpe himself. He mentioned that Norman Scott was known to him, and seemed to be reminding me of how far in print the law allows a newspaper to go. I had no intention of letting the newspaper go anywhere in the context that was implied.

Next, I had a private visit, at my home, from two journalists, Barrie Penrose and Roger Courtiour, whose names were to become very prominent in an unfolding drama and during the Old Bailey trial. Their investigations were published in their book, *The Pencourt File*, in 1978. This book appeared before any charges were brought against anyone. There was nothing I could say that would help these journalists.

At the time of the Exmoor incident few people in that area were aware that the Scott allegations had been known for some years to the top ranks of the Liberal, Conservative and Labour parties, to Fleet Street and to the Home Office. Checked by the risks of libel action, the national Press had remained silent.

. . . . . .

My newspaper had referred to the difficulty of obtaining information from the police about the Exmoor incident. I had a telephone call on this matter from Robin Maxwell-Hyslop, M.P. for the Tiverton division, who tabled a question in Parliament.

The Home Office Under-Secretary, Dr. Shirley Summerskill, denied that the department had instructed the Somerset and Avon

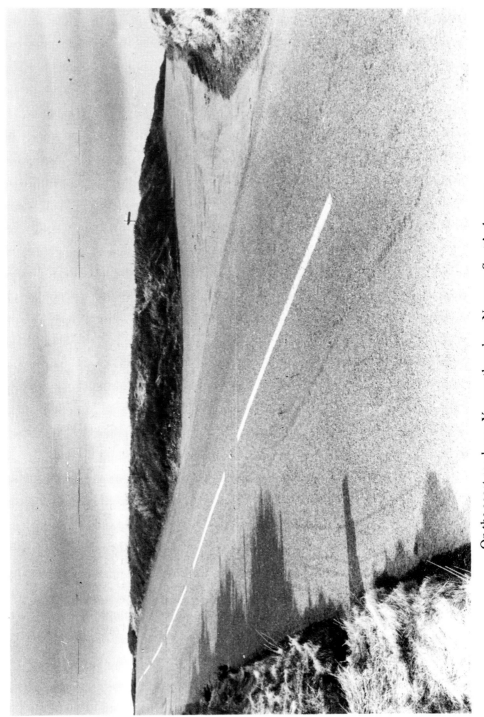

On the coast road near Yenworthy where Norman Scott's dog was

police to withhold information. but this did not satisfy the Tiverton M.P. He said it did not tally with what he had been told locally.

Mr. Maxwell-Hyslop had not yet done, and now the Exmoor mystery was to have a political undertone. This was a period in which the support of the Liberal Party was necessary to keep the Labour Government in office. Mr. Maxwell-Hyslop, a Conservative, now tabled a motion for the Commons. This recommended that in the Register of Members' Interests the categories should include 'Instances where the Home Office has intervened, officially or un-officially, to persuade provincial police forces to withhold from the Press information which would be damaging to the personal reputation of M.P.s on whose support (or lack of effective opposition) the continuation in office of the Government depends'.

Two events early in 1976 brought a simmering pot to the boil. Norman Scott, appearing at an industrial tribunal in Barnstaple, again gave vent to his allegations concerning Jeremy Thorpe. This time the Press was safe. It availed itself of court privilege and printed the allegations. These were now in the public eye for the first time.

Then in March, Andrew Gino Newton was tried at Exeter Crown Court on a charge of possessing a firearm with intent to endanger life. After the dog-shooting affair he had gone abroad. On his return, he was arrested at London Airport. Norman Scott, of course, gave evidence for the prosecution at the trial, but was manoeuvred away from his now familiar pattern of allegation.

The Press gathered in droves. They had been scenting what they thought might be an attempted murder for political reasons, and it is unlikely that they were foxed by Newton's surprise defence. This was that Scott had been blackmailing him over a nude photograph, and he (Newton) was intending to frighten Scott into returning the picture, thus ending the blackmail.

Newton said there had been no intention to endanger life. He subsequently admitted that his court story was untrue and that he had committed perjury. He was convicted on the firearm charge and given a prison sentence of two years.

Behind the scenes there was movement. The Director of Public Prosecutions had instructed the police to enquire into Norman Scott's allegations.

On May 10th Jeremy Thorpe resigned as Leader of the Liberal Party. On May 12th Harold Wilson, who had resigned as Prime Minister in March, invited Penrose and Courtiour, the journalists who had visited me, to expose 'a South African plot to discredit Jeremy Thorpe'. While still Prime Minister, Mr. Wilson had said in answer to a parliamentary question that he had no doubt that there was strong South African participation 'in recent activities relating to the Leader of the Liberal Party'. This was shadowy stuff. It may now be seen as a diversionary ploy.

.   .   .   .   .   .

Newton served only part of his prison sentence. He was released in April 1977. In October that year the smouldering Exmoor mystery flared up sensationally. Newton made allegations, which a daily newspaper printed, that a prominent member of the Liberal Party had hired him to murder Norman Scott.

The enquiry ordered by the Director of Public Prosecutions into the Scott allegations were begun by Chief Supt Proven Sharpe, of the Devon and Cornwall Constabulary, who interviewed Jeremy Thorpe at his North Devon home. Subsequently, the investigations were taken on by Det. Chief Supt. Michael Challes, of the Somerset and Avon C.I.D. He flew to America to interview Mr. Peter Bessell, former Liberal M.P. for Bodmin, and one-time close friend of Jeremy Thorpe. The outcome of these enquiries burst startlingly from TV screens and newspapers on August 4th, 1978.

Jeremy Thorpe, David Malcolm Holmes (former deputy treasurer of the Liberal Party), John Le Mesurier (a South Wales carpet dealer) and George Deakin (a South Wales club owner) were charged at Minehead 'that on divers dates between January 1st 1973 and November 18th, 1977, in the county of Devon and elsewhere, they conspired together and with others unknown to murder Norman Scott'. Later, Thorpe alone was charged 'that between January 1st, 1969 and March 30th, 1969 he unlawfully incited David Malcolm Holmes to murder Norman Scott'.

Former M.P. Peter Bessell was coming to England to be a principal witness in the Crown's case against his old friend and the three other men accused.

. . . . . .

Nationwide interest was focused upon Minehead Magistrates' Court on the morning of November 20th, 1978. Crowds gathered outside for a glimpse of the four defendants, but local people looked askance at those it held to be sensation seekers. Such was the demand for Press seats that these had to be allocated by ticket.

Normally, reporting would have been forbidden, these being merely committal proceedings, and so there was a gasp and a stir when the defendant Deakin applied for the lifting of the restriction on reporting. So the lid was coming off. The media prepared for a long stay, and hotels were said to be making a killing in accommodation. Some reporters arranged with private householders for the daily use of their telephones.

For the next three weeks lurid detail from 'the case of the century' was fed to the public as prosecution witnesses gave their evidence. The magistrates ruled that the prosecution had made out a *prima facie* case, and they committed the four defendants for trial. Thorpe then spoke for the first time: 'I plead not guilty and will vigorously defend this matter'.

Minehead emptied of its temporary residents, and the TV cameras vanished from the environs of the court. They would next appear in a political setting.

76

Early in 1979 the Labour Government's cliff-hanging to power with Liberal support ended in defeat on a vote of confidence, and a General Election was set for May 3rd.

The trial of the four defendants was to have opened on April 30th, but in view of Jeremy Thorpe's participation in the General Election campaign the Lord Chief Justice granted a deferment of the trial until May 8th.

Thorpe went gamely into his North Devon campaign, but the tide of success was generally surging towards the Conservative Party. Thorpe polled well—23,338—but his Conservative opponent polled better, and he lost the seat he had first won in 1959. Four days later he entered the dock of Number One Court at the Old Bailey with Deakin, Holmes and Le Mesurier. All pleaded not guilty.

.   .   .   .   .

Here is an outline of the prosecution's case as presented by Mr. Peter Taylor, Q.C., leading counsel for the Crown:

In the early 1960s Jeremy Thorpe had a homosexual relationship with Norman Scott, and thereafter Scott was a danger to his reputation and career. Scott pestered him for help and talked to others about the relationship. In 1967 Thorpe was elected Leader of the Liberal Party, and Scott continued to be a threat to his ambition. Thorpe's anxiety became an obsession which gave rise to desperation.

Early in 1969 Thorpe incited his friend, David Holmes, in the presence of Peter Bessell, M.P., to kill Scott. Holmes and Bessell tried to dissuade Thorpe; and other, less dramatic, measures were suggested.

In 1974, Scott, having gone to live in Thorpe's constituency, talked openly of his relationship with the Liberal Leader and said he was trying to publish a book about it. David Holmes became convinced that the only way to end the threat to Thorpe and the Liberal Party was to kill Scott.

Holmes knew John Le Mesurier in South Wales, and through him he met George Deakin. A plot was hatched to find someone who would kill Scott for reward. Deakin recruited Andrew Newton as the hired assassin, and both Deakin and Holmes briefed him.

The reward was to be £10,000. Unsuccessful attempts were made to lure Scott to his death, but in October 1975 Newton went to Devon, gained Scott's confidence and drove him out on to Exmoor. This was the night of the 24th. Newton produced a gun, shot Scott's dog, but failed to shoot Scott.

When Newton was released from gaol he was paid £5,000, half the contract price. It was handed over to him by Le Mesurier. The money was procured by Thorpe who persuaded Jack Hayward, a wealthy benefactor, to make a substantial contribution to Liberal election funds. Thorpe personally arranged for the money to be delivered by a devious route to Holmes so that payment could be made to Newton.

The full reporting of the Crown's startling evidence at the Minehead

77

Minehead Magistrates' Court

court robbed the trial itself of some of the drama it would otherwise have produced, but there was a general expectancy of the intense interest the evidence of the four defendants would arouse.

This was not to be. On the 21st day of the trial, when the Crown concluded its case, counsel for Thorpe, Holmes and Le Mesurier announced that these defendants would not give evidence, nor would any witnesses be called on their behalf. Deakin, however, did give evidence. He denied he had done anything beyond putting Newton in touch with Holmes.

Astonishing as was the decision not to put Thorpe, Holmes and Le Mesurier in the witness box, it had to be conceded that the cross-examination of the Crown's main witnesses, Bessell, Scott and Newton had done much to destroy their credibility. Additionally, the comments of the judge, Mr. Justice Cantley, in his summing-up and during the proceedings, seemed to cast further doubt on the veracity of the witnesses. With such phrases as 'liars and self-confessed perjurors' defence counsel did not fail to impress the jury, and the judge himself catalogued Scott as 'crook, fraud, sponger, whiner, parasite'.

There was particular interest in what Newton said about the Exmoor incident . . . that he had tried to frighten Scott with a bungled murder attempt, and that he had no intention of killing him. So, when he levelled the gun he pretended it jammed. However, a Home Office expert had given evidence that the gun was prone to jamming and had done so four times under test.

There was a surprise when Mr. John Matthew, Q.C., spoke for Holmes. He admitted the existence of a conspiracy to frighten Scott, and said Holmes had been ready to admit such a charge, had it been brought. But the evidence on the charge of conspiracy to murder 'defied belief'.

Yet Mr. Gareth Williams, Q.C., for Deakin, told the jury: 'On the evidence you would be perfectly entitled and logically consistent to convict Thorpe, Holmes and Le Mesurier and acquit Deakin'.

For Jeremy Thorpe, Mr. George Carman, Q.C., spoke of 'squalid witnesses called by the Crown'. He admitted, however, that Thorpe was a man of homosexual tendencies when first he met Scott.

The trial ended on June 22nd. The jury, who had been out for 52 hours, came back with a unanimous verdict of 'Not guilty' in respect of all defendants.

.   .   .   .   .

On Sunday, July 1st, nine days after the acquittal of the defendants, the parish church of Bratton Fleming, in the heartland of Jeremy Thorpe's former constituency, was the scene of a thanksgiving service. It was conducted by the incumbent, the Rev. John Hornby, who was also rural dean and chairman of the village Liberal Association.

In a reference to Jeremy Thorpe, Mr. Hornby said: 'Countless thousands of people in North Devon rise up and call him blessed.

By common consent, Jeremy has been the best **M.P. North Devon** has ever had or could have'.

Mr. Hornsby prayed that God would drive out from **human hearts** the evils of suspicion, hatred and, most of all, the self-righteousness of all those concerned in the recent trial at the **Old Bailey.** He also uttered a prayer of thankfulness for the deliverance of the **Thorpes** and their families from their ordeal.

. . . . . .

This was the last Exmoor echo of a single pistol shot. Whether Newton's gun really jammed for the next shot, or whether it was the man's pretence, will never be known, but Scott remained alive. The dog it was that died.